Get rid
DEM █S

It's your time to Shine!

Aliss Cresswell

Get rid of those demons

© Copyright 2023 – Aliss Cresswell

All Scripture quotations are taken from the New International Version © 1973, 1978, 1984, 2011 by International Bible Society unless otherwise stated.

ISBN 13: 9780957264281

Published by Spirit Lifestyle Ltd

More information and resources:
www.SpiritLifestyle.org

Testimonials

"I had sensory processing disorder for years after a traumatic incident as a child. My father tried to kill me and my whole family before I was two. I was unable to let anyone touch me ever since I was a little child and I made life hell for those around me. I was visited by demons, I had nightmares for decades. I couldn't stand music or wear certain materials. Sounds would trigger an attack so I couldn't go out to a restaurant or buy groceries. The slightest thing would startle me.

The condition kept me isolated and controlled my life. I didn't know it was caused by a demon until now! I realized it was a demon of control that wanted to control not just me but everyone around me. Aliss has helped me. The demons have left me and I feel like a weight has been lifted. I feel lighter, I feel better, I feel more in my own body. I feel good, I feel grounded. I'm free." AJ

"A lot of things happened to me in my life and I'd held all that pain in. As Aliss was talking about getting free from demons, my heart began to beat so fast. Then I knew I had to forgive and release it. I let go of all the fear and the dishonesty. I had no idea that I had any demons until today. I felt demons coming off me and out of me; they kept leaving. Now I know I'm free of all of that. Heaven opened up for me today and I pray for everyone else that the same will happen for you too." J

"I had addictions that had wrecked my life. Now they've all gone. My family say I'm a different person. Thank you!" CH

"I was diagnosed with psychosis but since discovering this teaching, I recognized the cause and I've been set free. My life has completely changed. Thank you Aliss." JH

"This has been so impactful. Now I have the power to take control over my thoughts. The debilitating anxiety, fear, confusion and stress have been replaced with calm, peace and happiness. The change is remarkable and now I'm enjoying my new life and freedom. This is the real me!" PT

About The Author

Aliss Cresswell believes in the God of miracles and living a life full of love and power. Through pioneering Miracle Cafés® and Spirit Lifestyle® training, Aliss and her husband Rob equip and activate those who pursue a Spirit-filled life to demonstrate God's power and transform communities around the world. Aliss is the author of many books including 'How to be Healed' and 'The Normal Supernatural Christian Life'. Aliss & Rob have been married for over three decades with adult children and grandchildren.

Follow @alisscresswell

Table of Contents

Introduction

I f you want to experience the love and power of God personally and live in the fullness of who you were created to be, then this book is for you.

Satan doesn't want you to know the truth. The Bible says that our enemy blinds the souls of people, like a veil over hearts and minds. This book has been written to expose these veils so that they can be removed, that you may know the truth and when you act upon it, the truth has the power to set you free.

It is your time to shine, and the devil has been doing whatever he can to prevent that from happening, even since before you were born. But things are about to change as you read on and discover what God has planned for your life. It is time for those veils to be removed.

This book reveals the truth and teaching on how to apply that truth to your own life and situations, thus releasing breakthrough. It also holds powerful spiritual principles that can bring fundamental changes to your thinking, your behavior and your relationships, that will in turn help you succeed and find fulfillment in every area of your life.

For many years it has been a passion of mine to see people set free and whole in spirit, soul and body, empowered to live the successful and fulfilled lives they were born for. My name means 'Sacred Flame'. As a baby, I was dedicated to Jesus, and the presiding Minister prophesied that I would be a messenger of the Gospel, a flame of fire. I am a messenger, and the message I bring is the good news of Jesus Christ and His heavenly kingdom realm, here on earth, for you and your loved ones, no matter who you are, what you've done or what has been done to you.

The good news about Jesus and how He demolished the power of Satan by His death on the cross and His subsequent resurrection, includes freedom from demons, freedom from torment and everything else the enemy is using to destroy your life and attempting to block you from fulfilling your destiny.

This book contains practical help, key principles to live by and is packed full of remarkable stories of real-life situations to help you understand how you can be free too. But above all, it delivers the supernatural power of God to set you free.

Read this book to help you identify the demonic influences affecting you or your loved ones and discover the truth that can transform your life. Through it, I offer you a key to unlock the prison door that holds you captive in areas of your life you may not even realize, but you are the only one who can make that choice for yourself and use the key.

I am presenting you with the truth from Scripture; it's up to you whether you believe that truth, take a step of faith, act upon it and apply it to your life.

It may help to read through this book more than once, or to pause and take notes. To get the most from this book, I encourage you to pray the prayers out loud. Don't rush, but take time to think through what you are praying and allow the power of God to set you free.

I ask that you be honest and let the light of the Holy Spirit shine into the darkest, secret places of your heart and into your life. God knows all about it anyway, but the more you open up to Him and share with Him your struggles, your guilt, your past sins and traumas, the more He is then able to help you, to forgive you and to bring freedom to every area of your life.

Imagine being diagnosed with something malign in your body, but not wanting to let that thing be taken out, and so it festers and eventually makes you much worse until it is exposed and removed. That is what can happen to us when evil spirits affect us, but we do nothing.

Or what if you had a huge weed in your garden? There would be no point to just hacking at the parts you can see, but leaving the root in. The weed will grow back, oftentimes bigger and spreading further, more quickly. The only way to be completely free is first to identify it as a weed and pull it out from the root so it is completely gone. That is what you can do with any demons coming against your life with the help of the truths contained within this book; identify them, expose the root and remove them completely. So what remains in your life is pure, lovely and fruitful, just like a beautiful garden coming into blossom, without the weeds that try to choke it or make it barren.

Maybe there are patterns of behavior that you can't seem to change. Or you're wondering if there is a curse on your life or on your family. You may be accident prone, have anxieties and fears, recurring health issues, bad thoughts, anger, voices in your head, other mental health problems or addictions. Or maybe something drives you or controls you and you can't stop. Heaviness, hopelessness, thoughts of suicide. All these are about to be exposed for what they are, so get ready to be free.

I don't need to be with you in person, but as you read out the prayers I have written and apply the principles in this book, then you can benefit from the same power of Jesus that I'm talking about. It's just as if He's in the room with you; in fact He is, even though you don't see Him.

I've tried to make this book practical and straight-forward, keeping things simple yet powerful so that there is no blockage to you receiving your full deliverance and ongoing freedom.

As you read, you may find yourself getting angry, falling asleep, feeling confused, a weird pain or some other unusual symptom. Recognize it as simply a demon that is getting twitchy because it is being exposed. Be encouraged that you will soon be free; in fact, if something begins to manifest while you're reading, just tell it to leave you and keep reading. You are getting your life back! In the following chapters I'll explain how you can be free and then we will pray together and help you as you are set free from all darkness and step fully into God's wonderful light and His peace.

Before you read this book, I encourage you to say the following prayer out loud:

"Father God, I ask that through your Son, Jesus, you would protect me from the evil one. That every evil spirit operating in my life would be bound and silenced from speaking or interfering as I read this book. Lord God, please speak to me clearly through your Holy Spirit and show me the truth. Please shine your light and expose every area of my life that is in darkness so that I can shine with your glory. I want to know the truth and be set free. In Jesus' name, Amen."

CHAPTER ONE

The Unveiling

"**D**EMONIAC" was the word I got when I asked the Holy Spirit to show me about the delivery guy who was about to arrive at my door. 'Oh, that's all I need,' I thought to myself. Immediately my mind went to the demoniac – a very demonized man - in the Bible, as I asked the Holy Spirit to show me more.

The first thing I remembered was that the guy in the gospel accounts would cut himself. So, when the delivery driver arrived, I told him that God had shown me something about him. Unfortunately, his van was blocking the road and was holding up a car, so we didn't have much time. But I asked him if he, or someone close to him, suffered with mental health issues and self-harm.

He told me that a young woman he knew, but hadn't seen in years, had just messaged him a few hours ago to say she wanted to hurt herself. She had a history of self-harm and apparently her arms were really messed up. He had no idea why she'd contacted him at four in the morning completely out of the blue!

In addition to this, he'd come all the way from a supermarket 65 miles away to bring our groceries, but he didn't understand why. God obviously wanted to get his attention.

After praying for the girl he'd mentioned to be set free, I started to prophesy to the guy and told him that he has God's heart of compassion and that he'll come into contact with more people like the young lady who need to know God's love and freedom; that as He follows Jesus, he will have the wisdom and the power to be able to help them. He was glad he'd come all this way.

He had to dash, but he stayed a moment to tell me, "I've never been into religion, but I want to come to faith. There's a SPIRITUAL WAR going on and the only option is faith."

This man is not the first 'random' person to tell me they're aware of a spiritual war going on in the world right now and they are turning to God because of it.

More and more people are becoming aware of the fact that spiritual forces are impacting our world and our everyday lives personally, and I guess that's why you've picked up this book. You know that there is more happening around you and to you than meets the eye, and you want to be empowered to do something about it.

I'm going to share something with you that has the potential to transform your world. It's quite simple, and the more we can understand what is happening spiritually, and act upon it, the more our lives and the lives of those around us will change for the better.

The Bible holds the key: **"The god of this age has blinded the minds of unbelievers so that they should not discern the truth, preventing them from seeing the illuminating light of the gospel that displays the glory of Christ, who is the image of God" (2 Corinthians 4:4).**

The god of this age is Satan, our enemy, who covers our minds and our souls with a veil so that we cannot know, see or understand the truth of who we are, what is going on around us and what our true inheritance is. The 'unseen' realm is eternal but the world we see around us is temporary: you don't need to look far – sickness, ageing, death, disease, bad news, war, famine, hatred, torment, loss. Even creation itself is cloaked with the ravages of decay.

Like the Matrix movie, people are born into a world they think is real, but they are living a sham of the truth. However once they know the truth, they can break free.

Here is our true inheritance and it is available to all: **"...Whenever anyone turns to the Lord (Jesus), the veil is taken away. Now the Lord is the Spirit, and where the Spirit of the Lord is, there is freedom. And we all, who with unveiled faces contemplate the Lord's glory, are being transformed into His image with ever-increasing glory, which comes from the Lord, who is the Spirit" (2 Corinthians 3:16-18).**

The devil will always challenge our identity and God's truth. At the beginning of the Bible we read how the enemy approached Adam and Eve in the garden and right away had them questioning what God had said as well as their inheritance and their identity in Him. **"Did God really say...?"** (see Genesis 3). The enemy continues to do this today with each one of us. His aim is to deceive us into believing lies about God and about ourselves and undermining our true identity and inheritance. He wants to keep us in the dark.

He attempts, often successfully, to deceive each one of us in different ways. He knows our weak points and how we have been taught or brought up to view the world. The enemy has blinded your mind so you have been unable to know the truth. He has deceived you into thinking that what you see and experience in the natural realm is the truth, when it is not.

But God sent His Son Jesus Christ into the world to set us free from the power of the devil. As Jesus hung on the cross and gave up His spirit, the thick veil in the temple that separated the most holy place (God's presence) from the rest of the temple was torn from top to bottom.

"On this mountain He (God) will destroy the shroud that enfolds all peoples, the sheet that covers all nations..." (Isaiah 25:7).

VEILS OF DECEPTION ARE BEING REMOVED

Many years ago when the Holy Spirit was revealing this to me, something happened that confirmed what I was learning. Our beautiful daughter was brought up in our loving Christian home but when she was seventeen, the Holy Spirit showed me that she was seeing a guy who was a lot older, like in his thirties. I also got the distinct impression that he had been living on the streets, got into fights and was actually a drug dealer. When I initially asked her if she was seeing someone, she denied it, but as I began to describe the guy and what the Lord had shown me, she reluctantly admitted to it.

Soon after this, she went out one night and didn't come home. She was gone for around six months altogether. We had no idea where she was or who this guy was. As you can imagine, we were very concerned for her. But I chose not to worry and I said to the Lord, "She's your daughter – I commit her into your hands and I trust that you will protect her. Please show me how to pray."

Rather than praying for her and the dealer to split up, I wanted to pray exactly in line with the Holy Spirit. I thought, what if they both are supposed to be together, that they are going to get radically saved and change the world for Jesus? 'Not my will Lord but yours be done.' A difficult decision as a mother, but one that I'm glad I took. I prayed that God's kingdom would come to both of them.

I kept trusting God's protection of her and one day I clearly sensed the Lord showing me to pray this: "I take authority over the 'veil' of deception that the enemy has placed over her mind and I command it be removed through the power and the blood of Jesus. That she would know the truth and the truth will set her free. It's time to come home."

Amazingly, she phoned me, almost straight away. "Mum – come and pick me up. I want to come home." Later, as she sat in the car in floods of tears next to me, she blurted out, "I've been so stupid. I'm so sorry. I don't know what came over me. It's like I was blinded to the truth of what I was doing. I couldn't see what he was really like but today something seemed to leave my mind and I could clearly see the truth. I thought, what am I doing with this ugly, 'old' drug dealer!? I want to go home."

She'd been living in a dreadful situation – instead of her loving family and comfortable home that was available to her, she'd been 'blinded' by the enemy, lost her true identity and was living well below her potential in squalor and being badly treated.

There are some lessons to learn here. One is that we need to pray in accordance with God's will and not our own controlling or manipulating prayers out of anxiety, fear or our own desires. But the main point I want you to understand is that you are a child of God, a co-heir with Jesus Christ – all that He has and is, is yours.

The enemy has tried to blind your mind and your understanding with a thick veil so that you are unable to know who you really are - your true worth and value to God and what your purpose is - so that you are unable to live in the fullness of God's glory and freedom and peace. But I want to tell you that it is time for you to shine. The real you, without the veil of darkness and oppression and fear.

Satan has blinded our minds with 'veils' of deception so that we cannot understand nor therefore live in the fullness of our glorious inheritance that has been made available to us through Jesus. And through this book my aim is to expose the deception and therefore help you remove those veils so that you can know the truth that will set you free and transform your world!

CHAPTER TWO

The Power Of
The Spirit Realm

The spirit realm is more powerful than the physical, natural realm. Just because we can't always see the spirit realm with our natural eyes doesn't mean that it isn't real. What happens in the spirit realm directly impacts the earthly realm where we live. If we can understand this principle of life, then it will help empower us enormously. However, there are conflicting powers that operate in the spirit realm that we also must understand.

Think about the laws of the universe such as the law of gravity which affects us every day. Without gravity we would be weightless and the moon would collide with the sun and so on. The loss of gravity would have a devastating impact, but you cannot see it with your physical eyes. Or take air waves, the medium through which radio and TV signals are transmitted, or the internet. They are all invisible to the naked eye but most definitely real and have an affect on our lives. This is also the case with demons.

THE TRUTH ABOUT DEMONS

I am no expert on demons, and I don't want to be! But over the years I have encountered demons so many times in other people and in my own life that I have come to recognize some of their traits. The Bible tells us the truth about demons and shows us some of the ways in which they operate. However, as C.S. Lewis, the Oxford scholar and author of the Narnia books wrote in 'The Screwtape Letters': "There are two equal and opposite errors into which our race can fall about the devils (demons). One is to disbelieve in their existence, the other is to believe and to feel an unhealthy interest in them!"

We don't want to make the mistake of focussing on demons, but we do need to be aware that, even though we don't always see them with our physical eyes, evil spirits are real. We may not have been aware of them in the past, but it doesn't mean that they haven't been wreaking havoc in our lives.

It's important not to focus on demons. Do not fear demons; the fear of demons is from the demons themselves. We must have our eyes fixed on Jesus and His kingdom, **"...in order that Satan might not outwit us. For we are not unaware of his schemes"**

(2 Corinthians 2:11). It is a mistake to completely ignore the enemy or to believe that he does not exist.

Ephesians 6:12 states, **"For our struggle is not against flesh and blood, but against the rulers, against the authorities, against the powers of this dark world and against the spiritual forces of evil in the heavenly realms."**

In writing this book, I have been careful to keep a balance between helping you to be aware of the enemy's schemes and ways in which he tries to affect your life negatively, but more importantly, focussing on Jesus as the light and the fact that He has overcome all the powers of darkness.

Some years ago, I was speaking at one of our workshops, and during the Q&A session a woman asked a question about deliverance from demons. She told us how she was struggling to be free and wanted some insight. Immediately the Holy Spirit showed me that she'd been reading 'Christian' books on demons by a certain Christian 'deliverance' minister. I asked if she'd read any of these and she replied, "Oh yes, I regularly read all her books!" I explained how that was the problem. Those books almost glorified the enemy by sharing many stories of demonic activity, and the result from reading them had brought fear and empowered the enemy in her life. As I told her this, she began to lurch backwards and forwards as the demonic forces within her manifested, confirming what I'd just discerned. Thankfully, she got fully free once she'd received the revelation of the source of those evil spirits and broke agreement with them.

The more we focus on Jesus, the more we will be like Him and radiate His light and glory, and continue to walk in His freedom.

"Christ's resurrection is your resurrection too. This is why we are to yearn for all that is above, for that's where Christ sits enthroned at the place of all power, honor, and authority. Feast on all the treasures of the heavenly realm and fill your thoughts with heavenly realities, and not with the distractions of the natural realm" (Colossians 3:1,2 TPT).

GOD'S KINGDOM

Jesus spoke many times about God's kingdom realm of heaven. So what is the kingdom of God? It is the 'King's domain', where He rules and reigns. In God's kingdom realm of heaven there is no death, no pain, no sin, no disease. When Jesus walked the earth, His disciples witnessed the kingdom of heaven in miraculous healings, casting out demons, weather miracles, resurrecting people from the dead and so on.

Jesus taught His followers to pray, **"Our Father who is in heaven, holy is your name. Your kingdom come,**

28

your will be done on earth as it is in heaven..." As God's kingdom comes to earth we see demons displaced, the sick healed, lives transformed and many other types of incredible miracles.

Well, I have got to tell you that God's kingdom realm of heaven is here. Now. On earth and available for you today. Jesus said, **"The kingdom of God is within and among you because of my presence" (Luke 17:21 AMP).**

POPULAR MISCONCEPTIONS ABOUT DEMONS

I did a search on the internet and it's amazing to see what people think demons are. Many people think that by using certain tools or particular rituals they can get rid of demons but I want to be clear that these methods will not help you: Herbs such as sage will not help banish demons. Neither will wafting smoke around, using crystals, chanting, banging pots and pans or even inviting a medium or spiritualist to 'cleanse' you or your home. This is likely to make matters worse.

Many people think that you can be rid of demons by controlling your negative energy, thoughts and emotions. Of course, making right choices about how we think, speak and behave will help prevent evil spirits coming in, but it won't necessarily get rid of them.

By reading this book you'll gain a clear understanding of what demons are, discover if you have them in your life, your home or in the lives of those around you and find out the only sure way to be free from them. And most importantly, if you follow the advice in this book then you should be able to get completely free very quickly and remain free, as well as help others to do the same!

POSSESSED OR DEMONIZED?

The word 'demon' appears many times in the Bible and is translated from the original Greek word 'daimonion' which is derived from the word 'daimon'. Some translations of the Bible use the expression 'demon possessed'. This seems to indicate that the person is fully taken over by a demon, which in some cases they may be. However, according to the late Derek Prince, a Christian Minister and Bible scholar who helped a lot of people recognize and get free from demons over the past few decades, the word 'demonized' is more accurate than 'possessed'. He explained that 'demonized' is closer to the original Greek word and it is helpful to use this, as there are different degrees of demonization, whereas possession indicates being fully taken over by a demon. You may not be possessed by a demon or demons, but you may be demonized to some degree and not even aware of it!

CAN CHRISTIANS NEED DELIVERANCE FROM DEMONS?

This is one question that we get asked time and time again. Many Christians cannot believe that a demon and the Holy Spirit can inhabit the same person or that a Christian, protected by the blood of Jesus, can allow a demon to enter their life.

However, I have come across hundreds and probably more accurately, thousands of people professing to be Christian, who have given their lives to Jesus and been baptized, who have been set free from evil spirits, some dramatically. But we must also base our answer on the word of God. So let's take a look at that:

In Acts 8 we read that Philip was in Samaria and he was preaching the good news of Jesus. The Bible states that as he did so, demons were leaving people, they were healed, giving their lives to Jesus and being baptized. These people were being delivered from evil spirits at the same time they chose to follow Jesus, but what if someone asks Jesus into their life and they do not receive deliverance at the same time? What happens to those demons? At some point, they will need to be set free. It was common in the early church for people to receive deliverance from demons at the same time they chose to follow Jesus and be baptized. Since this rarely seems to happen in our day, then it stands to reason that there must be a lot of Christians who still need deliverance. Sometimes demons leave automatically, but very often they need to be recognized for what they are and driven out.

"The devil prowls around like a roaring lion seeking whom to devour..." (1 Peter 5:8-9). Evil spirits, working on behalf of the enemy, are searching for people whom they can enter. Jesus said that the thief comes to steal, kill and destroy His sheep. We are His sheep. We are not immune to the devil, and we must be on our guard and know what to do to repel the advances of the enemy. If we do not, evil spirits can come into our lives, even uninvited, and they will stay and cause havoc, attracting other demons to themselves, until we get a revelation of the truth and command them to leave through the power of Jesus.

We video interviewed a Christian woman after she was dramatically set free from evil spirits at one of our workshops. She had attended a local church for many years. She said, "During the session on deliverance when Aliss was talking about getting free from demons, my heart began to beat so fast. I felt like something was trying to choke me then a pain went down into my arm. In my mind I heard the demon say it would shut me up and if I spoke it would hurt me.

My stomach was cramping so badly and then I kept coughing even though I was trying not to. But I wanted to get that thing out of me. Then I felt demons coming off me and out of me; they kept leaving.

A lot of things have happened to me in my life and I'd held all that in. Then I knew I had to forgive and release it. I let go of all the fear and the dishonesty. Now I know I'm free of all of that. I've been a Christian for years. I thank God that I am now free and I want to help other people get free from demons too. I had no idea that I had any demons until today.

Last night I was coughing because those demons knew I was coming today but nothing was going to stop me. Everything seemed to go wrong and tried to stop me but I was determined. Heaven opened up for me today and I pray for everyone else that the same will happen for you too. I was making a lot of noise as they came out – the more I wanted them out, the more they wanted to stay in. But now I am completely free."

WHAT IS A DEMON AND WHAT POWER DO THEY HAVE?

When we look at the life of Jesus in the gospels it's clear that He not only believed in the existence of evil spirits, He actually spoke to them and taught us how to deal with them too.

When Jesus came near to people, demons would often manifest themselves. They spoke to Jesus, recognized who He was and often asked for mercy.

Mark 3:11 says: **"Whenever the impure spirits saw Him, they fell down before Him and cried out, "You are the Son of God."**

And in Matthew 8:29: **"What do you want with us, Son of God?" they shouted. "Have you come here to torture us before the appointed time?"**

Now that's interesting isn't it: **"…torture us before the appointed time…?"** What were they talking about? The Bible tells us that the fires of hell were created, not for people, but for Satan and his demonic angels (see Matthew 25:41). The demons knew that Jesus, as The Anointed One of God (The Christ), was the person who would ultimately judge and send them there. So, here's a good thing to remember about demons: God has already arranged for their destruction! What they are doing here on earth is simply trying to do as much damage as possible before they go there.

Reading the stories about demons in the Bible it's clear that these evil spirits ultimately want to destroy the people they are tormenting. They are disembodied spirits who are seeking to '**kill, steal and destroy' (John 10:10)** through influencing people's thoughts and behavior.

In Mark chapter 5 we read the story of a demonized man who lived in a graveyard bound in chains. The evil spirits would cause him to cry out and cut himself with stones. However as soon as Jesus arrived on the scene, the evil spirits had to do what Jesus said. They had to submit to the power and authority of Jesus and leave the tormented man until he was sitting there, **"dressed and in his right mind" (Mark 5:15).**

CAN A CHRISTIAN BE INFLUENCED BY DEMONS?

Can a Christian be influenced by demons? Or are we protected from them no matter what we do? The reality is that though we may have the presence of the Holy Spirit in our lives, God still gives us free will. Since we can grieve or quench the Holy Spirit (1 Thessalonians 5:19, Ephesians 4:30) then our behavior can certainly affect our spiritual protection; to think otherwise would be foolish.

Now, I don't believe a follower of Jesus should or need have this kind of troubling spirit, but there are certain ways in which we can allow them to have power in our lives.

Here's a useful analogy for this spiritual principle: The physical world is full of microscopic germs that can harm our physical bodies. They are everywhere and given an opportunity, they will find a nice warm body and infect it or influence it. Though we can't see these germs we don't need to be afraid of them if we are living sensibly and looking after ourselves. That's why we should take the trouble to maintain a healthy lifestyle because it will protect us from the most common germs and they can do us no harm. In the same way, though demons are real and just a fact of life, they need not bother us at all if we take care of our spiritual health.

If you were to go out in England for a hike in the hills wearing nothing but a T shirt and shorts on a rainy day in February, very few would have sympathy for you if you caught a bad cold. They would say you'd been foolish. In the same way, the New Testament describes certain activities as detrimental to our spiritual health; they are foolish activities because they are going to harm our relationship with God and in this way make us susceptible to demonic influence.

Author Francis Frangipane teaches how the devil's legitimate domain is darkness. The book of Jude tells us, "And angels who did not keep their own domain, but abandoned their proper abode, He has kept in eternal bonds under darkness for the judgment of the great day" (Jude 6). Francis explains that these beings dwell in this moral darkness which is also the absence of God's manifest presence. Wherever there is willful disobedience to the Word of God, there is spiritual darkness and the potential for demonic activity. The devil can appear in any area of darkness, even the darkness that still exists in a Christian's heart.

HOW CAN I RECOGNIZE A DEMON?

Demons show all the hallmarks of a person with a personality. They seem to show emotion, they can speak, even make decisions: **"I will return to the house I left" (Matthew 12:44).**

Demons can tremble with fear: **"You believe that there is one God. Good! Even the demons believe that—and tremble" (James 2:19).** Often a person who has a spirit of fear will shake with fear; sometimes this happens during a panic attack which is a clear example of a spirit of fear manifesting. Or an accusing spirit may cause the person to shake as they are accusing someone.

Demons have knowledge. The demons knew the identity of Jesus before His disciples fully understood who He was: **"I know who you are—the Holy One of God!" (Mark 1:24)** and the demon that spoke to Jesus in Mark 5:9 knew that many other demons also resided in the man before they left at the command of Jesus.

Demons can speak. They sometimes seem to use the vocal chords of the person or animal they're indwelling. I once prayed for a guy who came into our Blacon café and as I did so, he spoke in a voice that was not his own. The demon exclaimed through him in a high screeching voice, repeatedly saying, "You've got the power of God! You've got the power of God!" I replied calmly, "Yes I know. Come out of him in the name of Jesus" at which the demon had to leave instantly. Then the man invited Jesus into his life.

I also heard a story from a friend about a guy who was living with his partner, a witch. As time went by, the guy gave his life to Jesus and invited a group of Christians round to his house. The pet cat that belonged to the witch spoke in a strangely human voice and demanded to know what the Christians were doing in its house! Needless to say, the man got out of the house and that relationship as fast as he could and went on to become a church leader and a police officer where he was able to help many people through spiritual discernment.

Demons work on behalf of Satan. In Luke 13:11, Jesus states that Satan had bound the disabled woman causing her to be bent over for eighteen years. But it was an evil spirit of infirmity Jesus cast out of her, and that resulted in her instant healing.

Demons have no body of their own and seek to inhabit the bodies of humans, or failing that, the bodies of animals or birds. In the Biblical encounter of Luke 8:32-33 we read that Jesus drove many demons out of a man and the demons then asked Him if they could enter a nearby herd of pigs. Jesus allowed them to do so, which caused the pigs to stampede into the sea and drown, causing uproar in that region.

PAY ATTENTION

It's important to recognize the different ways that demons operate against you. As already mentioned, they are spirits without a body, and often look to inhabit a person, or an animal or bird.

A few years ago, a friend of mine came to my house for a coffee. Suddenly, something strange happened; we both experienced identical symptoms: dizziness, a migraine-type headache, temporary deafness and blurred vision. I could only see half my friend's face - it was very strange. We recognized that it was evil spirits at work, so we prayed together and told them to leave. Most of the symptoms left immediately, apart from the pain in my head, which seemed to intensify.

I knew it was an evil spirit that was causing it, so after my friend left, I stood up and sternly told it to leave at the name of Jesus. As I did so, there was a loud bang on an upstairs window and a woodpecker fell to the ground, obviously dead, outside the patio window near where I was standing. I was astonished.

The migraine headache was gone but I realized that the evil spirit that had come at me must have left me, entered the woodpecker and caused it to die. The bird was on its back with its legs in the air, it looked very dead as though it had broken its neck. I wanted to resurrect it from the dead but wondered if I was supposed to lay hands on it as I really didn't fancy touching a dead bird! I was debating this for a few minutes before I did anything.

I remained inside, looking through the patio windows and didn't touch it, but I spoke out loud and said, "I command the spirit of death to leave this bird now, in Jesus' name." Instantly the bird's body came back to life, its broken neck straightened, it turned right side up and stood, blinking its eyes at me and then a little while later flew off. I was like, "Yes, my first resurrection!"

Demons have passions, lusts and emotions that they seek to vent through the bodies of humans. They work for Satan, our enemy. Jesus said that Satan comes to 'kill, steal and destroy' (John 10:10) and the evil spirits aim to do that on his behalf. They cause torment, pain and deception in people's lives and by reading this book you will begin to understand how they have been trying to destroy your life and the lives of those around you. Keep reading, as I'm going to help you identify the demons that have been coming against you and then help you to get free and stay free.

Jot down anything that strikes a chord with you as you're reading, because the Holy Spirit will be revealing things from the past as we go along. Get ready for your life to change dramatically!

THE ORIGIN OF DEMONS

The Bible is not clear as to where evil spirits originate. Some consider them to be fallen angels that were sent to earth along with Satan when he rebelled against God and was banished to earth. Others think they may originate from a pre-Adamic race or from some other source, but either way, we know that they do Satan's bidding. We must not forget, that even though they seem to be controlled by Satan, even Satan himself is simply a created being, way below the incredible power of Almighty God – Father, Son and Holy Spirit.

Not everything negative is a demon. It could be our own sinful thoughts or actions, our own self or our fallen nature that is to blame. The Bible tells us to 'put to death' our sinful nature and to consider ourselves dead but it tells us to 'cast out' demons. This is important as we need to 'crucify' the sinful nature and 'cast out' a demon. We cannot crucify a demon and cast out our sinful nature!

It is also important to hate that demonic thing and be single-minded about getting rid of it. Many people say they want to be free, but actually they have got used to their own behavior or thought process or illness, and deep down, they don't really want to let go of that lifestyle or for things to change.

For example, the Bible says that the devil is the father of lies. Evil spirits lie to us, however, sometimes we make friends with the lie. Sometimes the things that make us miserable are also pleasurable on some level. A hypochondriac (someone who is abnormally anxious about their health) may make people sympathetic and express concern for them. But the reality is, we don't have to be ill or in pain to receive love and affection. Perhaps a childhood association is that our parents only showed us affection when we were ill, but now we can discover that we have inherent value and worth in Christ. We are loved unconditionally by our Heavenly Father. As we receive that love, we can be set free.

Derek Prince wisely said that the Lord will deliver us from our enemies, but not our friends! It is important to be sure that we want to be totally free of evil spirits before we can get free.

I heard this story once from a family friend who was a Minister. Someone had come to him and asked, "Please cast out the spirit of laziness from me", to which our friend replied, "Bend over and I'll give you a kick up the backside! It isn't a demon, it's just that you're lazy." This might sound harsh, but the sentiment remains; you cannot cast out a demon that is simply your poor behavior. Having said that, there probably is a demon connected with laziness and since we can invite demons into our lives if we continue to behave badly, this man who was acting in a lazy way may unconsciously have invited a demon of tiredness, lethargy, fatigue or slothfulness to take up residence in his life.

THE DARK RULER OF THE EARTHLY REALM

Here's some straight talking from the Bible: **"You were once like corpses, dead in your sins and offenses. It wasn't that long ago that you lived in the religion, customs, and values of this world, obeying the dark ruler of the earthly realm who fills the atmosphere with his authority, and works diligently in the hearts of those who are disobedient to the truth of God. The corruption that was in us from birth was expressed through the deeds and desires of our self-life. We lived by whatever natural cravings and thoughts our minds dictated, living as rebellious children subject to God's wrath like everyone else"** (Ephesians 2:1-3 TPT).

Perhaps that speaks of your life now, even in just one or two areas. If we follow the ways of this world, going our own way, just pleasing ourselves, or seeking after all that the world offers, then what results is a dead-end existence, without fulfillment in life and with lack of real joy and peace. This verse clearly shows how Satan, the evil ruler of the earthly realm is at work in the lives of many. It's no wonder that the world is in such a state.

When we live according to the natural cravings and thoughts of our mind, we're rebelling against God and coming into agreement with the dark ruler of this natural world, Satan. This in turn makes our life subject to his rule and his power against us. It's time to choose whether we're going to be obedient to him and his calamitous plan for our life or submit to Father God and His wonderful plan and destiny for us, as His child and legal heir of all that He is and has.

We'll be looking at how you can put a stop to Satan's power in your life in the next chapters, but for now I want to help you see clearly what is really going on around you and clarify the choices and decisions you can make to bring change.

In John 8:44 TPT, Jesus states that the devil has **"been a murderer right from the start! He never stood with the truth, for he's full of nothing but lies—lying is his native tongue. He is a master of deception and the father of lies!"**

The word here for devil in the original Greek text means slanderer, accuser. In Aramaic which is the language Jesus spoke, it means adversary, taken from a root word that means to ridicule or gnaw. Have you ever felt something gnawing away at your life, your health, your finances, your relationships? I remember one time that someone prophesied to me and he could see in the spirit that something like a jackal was trying to gnaw away at my life. He bound that thing and released the fire of the Holy Spirit to burn it up and scare it away. Living close to God, wrapped in His love and His peace releases the fire of His presence and does not allow any demonic spiritual beings to come near.

CHAPTER THREE

Body, Soul And Spirit

L et's shine the light of Jesus and expose the dark places where the enemy tries to affect our lives. It's helpful to see where the root of the problem is so we can remove it. Then in later chapters we will cover how to deal with those spirits, and more importantly, how to live free and stay free of them.

Every person has a spirit, a soul and a body and so we will look at these in turn and discover some ways that the enemy affects us in each area of our lives.

HOW DEMONS AFFECT OUR PHYSICAL BODIES

In the last century, John G Lake was known for incredible miracles of healing and even resurrections from the dead. All his life he had witnessed many deaths and illnesses in his family right up to the point where his wife lay dying. He was so desperate and angry at the sickness around him that he threw his Bible down in exasperation. Picking it up, his eyes were drawn to this verse that lay on the open page where it had landed:

"God anointed Jesus of Nazareth with the Holy Spirit and with power: who went about doing good and healing all that were oppressed by the devil; for God was with Him" (Acts 10:38).

John later stated: "Like a flash from the blue, these words pierced my heart: Oppressed of the devil! So, God was not the author of sickness! And the people whom Jesus healed had not been made sick by God! Then I read the words of Jesus in Luke 13:16: "Ought not this woman... whom Satan has bound for eighteen years, be set free?" Once again Jesus attributed sickness to the devil. What a faith sprang up in my heart! What a flame of knowledge concerning the Word of God and the ministry of Jesus went over my soul! I saw as never before why Jesus healed the sick: He was doing the will of His Father; and in doing His Father's will, He was destroying the works of the devil." (see Hebrews 2:14).

After John read these Scriptures, he and his friends prayed with faith for his dying wife. She was miraculously healed as the power of God came upon her. She got up and said, "Praise God! I am healed!"

We see in the passage from Luke 13 above, that it was an evil spirit of infirmity, a demon, that had caused the woman's crippling back condition. Jesus simply commanded the spirit of infirmity to leave and the woman was instantly healed.

Hundreds of times we have also seen people instantly healed as a demon was told to leave and the power of Jesus released. (I don't have space to share them all here, but my book, 'How to be healed and stay healed' has many examples of this, as does our online portal SpiritLifestyle.com where you can see real-life transformation stories.)

YOU CAN LIVE PAIN FREE!

When considering the body in terms of how it is affected by the demonic, a common manifestation is that of chronic pain (often incurable by conventional medicine). For this reason, and the fact that pain affects so many, I'm going to focus on this issue here whilst also touching on many other common links between tormenting spirits and physical maladies.

Chronic primary pain is defined by the UK's National Health Service as persistent pain that continues for longer than 12 weeks despite medication or treatment. According to the UK government body NICE (National Institute of Health and Care Excellence) chronic pain is a condition which "can't be accounted for by another diagnosis" and accounts for up to a staggering 45% of all GP doctor appointments.

Incredibly, according to the NHS, half of all new visits to hospital clinics in the UK are made by people with chronic pain that has no apparent cause. This is likely to be a similar figure in many other nations. In fact, it is estimated that up to 40% of people within the US live with chronic pain (cited by the Center for Disease Control and Prevention, 2018 study).

UNEXPLAINED PAIN

Most people get back to normal following an injury or operation. But sometimes the pain carries on for longer even when the injury or surgical procedure has healed. Doctors are often baffled as to the longevity of the pain.

One lady I met told me she had chronic pain that resulted from major back surgery. She would spend weeks unable to stand and had to crawl to the bathroom and was often in floods of tears. No amount of medication seemed to help and she had put up with this for many years. It had caused misery not only for herself, but also her husband who had to look after her.

Chronic pain can also appear without any history of an injury or operation. For no apparent reason and without cause, pain is experienced by many people and is very real. These symptoms are sometimes known as "medically unexplained symptoms" when they last for more than a few weeks, and doctors cannot find a problem within the body that may be the cause. This doesn't mean the symptoms are faked or "all in the head" – they're real and can affect a person's ability to function properly. In some cases the pain is so bad that the person is unable to walk and may need to use a wheelchair or walking aids, or may be confined to bed. A recent BBC News article cited that a staggering one in four people live with chronic pain in the UK.

Not understanding the cause can make chronic pain even more distressing and difficult to cope with.

WHAT IS THE DIAGNOSIS?

Many people suffering from chronic pain are diagnosed with fibromyalgia, hormonal issues, chronic fatigue, virus complications, migraine headaches, ME and such like. Without an obvious cause, there is little that a medical professional can do.

WHAT IS REALLY THE CAUSE?

Traditionally, doctors have treated conditions based on either a physiological or mental health cause. However, every human consists of a spirit, soul and body (soul being the mind, emotions and will). We are complex creatures and there is more to us than simply what you can see with the eye. In traditional pharmaceutical medicine, doctors do not consider the spiritual aspect of the human being, but for thousands of years it has been well known that the spiritual aspect of a person is very real and has a strong bearing on the person as a whole. We cannot treat just one part of a person without it affecting another.

The reason that up to half of the population experiences unexplained physical pain is that many root causes of pain are in fact spiritual. The Bible makes it clear that the spirit realm has a powerful influence on the physical (see Ephesians 6).

IS THERE A CURE?

For years, doctors have prescribed common painkillers for patients with chronic pain, targeting the physical symptoms rather than the root cause. Increasingly, patients are turning to alternative forms of medicine and healthcare. Indeed, even the BBC recently reported that the UK government body NICE has advised doctors nationwide not to prescribe common painkillers any longer for chronic pain, including paracetamol and ibuprofen, due to long term use being harmful physically. Almost all types of medication, including painkillers, do have side-effects. Surprisingly though, NICE recommends antidepressants, acupuncture or psychological therapy instead.

HOW SAFE OR EFFECTIVE ARE ALTERNATIVE FORMS OF TREATMENT?

So if the government health body for the UK advises against common over-the-counter painkillers for chronic pain, which, it says, provides little evidence they help anyway, let's look at the alternatives it suggests.

Antidepressants may seem like a good solution if the person experiencing chronic pain is showing signs of depression due to the constant pain, which is understandable. However, evidence is clear that the side-effects of taking antidepressants are many and according to the NHS website (www.nhs.uk) can include anxiety, shaking, stomach problems, sexual problems, insomnia, blurred vision, problems urinating, tiredness, weight gain, excessive sweating, heart problems, twitching, diabetes, seizures, psychosis, stopping breathing, coma, suicidal thoughts, and if that wasn't enough, even muscle pain and headaches, presumably the very problems that one was attempting to alleviate in the first place!

HOW SAFE AND EFFECTIVE IS ACUPUNCTURE?

According to the NHS, 'Acupuncture is a treatment derived from ancient Chinese medicine. Fine needles are inserted at certain sites in the body. Traditional acupuncture is based on the belief that an energy, or "life force" flows through the body in channels called meridians. This life force is known as Qi (pronounced "chee").' When looking at any alternative therapy that includes 'energy' or 'life force' it is important to consider where the source of that energy or force originates. According to the Christian Bible, there are a number of forces at play in the world, and the highest force or power belongs to Jesus Christ (see Matthew 28).

Alternative practices that are rooted in Eastern religions do not recognize the power source as being Jesus Christ. Therefore, the power is either counterfeit or at best limited. In my book 'How To Be Healed and Stay Healed' I cite a former Oriental medicine advocate and teacher who unfortunately after being involved in these practices, subjected herself to the influence of evil spirits. Thankfully when she realized her mistake, she was set free from these spirits by the power of Jesus and her life was transformed.

The third suggestion from NICE, Psychological Therapy, is also known as 'talking therapies' and is where, in a safe space, the patient is encouraged to talk about their difficulties, in this case, the chronic pain experienced. Presumably by talking about your pain and the way it affects your life, this can help you come to terms with it. However, it is unable to remove that pain or cure it.

GETTING TO THE ROOT

So, let's look at what really is causing the pain in your body and how you can be cured. Let's go back to the fact that you consist of a body, a spirit and a soul (your mind, emotions and will) and that they are all connected. If you go to the doctor because you have a pain and the doctor diagnoses a large splinter in your body, then the doctor will remove that splinter which is the root cause, and the symptoms ie the pain, will leave. You can treat the symptoms, the pain, but until that splinter is gone, the pain will still be there. It's very similar with a spiritual cause. You have pain in your body and if the cause is spiritual, then you need to discover what that is and remove it. Then the pain will go.

Many chronic pain problems, even those that originate with some sort of injury or surgery, may in fact be spiritual. Evil spirits are all around and they like to try and enter our lives. They seem to be able to enter when our guard is down, such as during a traumatic experience, or if we come into agreement with them in any way, such as through a sinful behavior or simply by believing what they tell us. It's like we open a door to our lives – into our emotions, our mind, our body or our spirit, and in they come. Very often these evil spirits are spirits of pain or will bring a spirit of pain with them. Because they entered during a time of trauma in our lives or illness, it's important to break any agreement with them and give them their marching orders.

DOES IT REALLY WORK?

I mentioned earlier the lady who suffered from chronic pain due to major back surgery. As she shared her problem with me, the Holy Spirit showed me that there was no longer a physical problem with her back, but lying spirits were causing the pain, manifesting physically and robbing her of a full life. I told her to jump up quickly from her chair. She looked surprised and said there was no way she could do that. Again, I repeated, "It's just evil spirits, stand up in the name of Jesus." Amazingly, she took me at my word and jumped up from her chair and began walking up and down the main street. Faster and faster she went until she was laughing and telling me and all those around us that she had no pain. She was virtually running. Her life was transformed as a result and she went on to live a perfectly normal, pain-free life after that.

And in case you think you need someone like me to be with you in person to get free, all you need is the revelation of truth from Jesus.

Another lady had severe back pain and she emailed us to let us know what happened after watching one of our videos about evil spirits being a cause of pain and how to get free. She told us, "My back had been feeling very achy, strained and stressed. We spent the last four months sailing the Caribbean on our monohull. I also developed a foot cramp in my arch. Well, during your teaching, the pain in my back just melted away and the cramp in my foot left at the same time." She is just one of thousands of people who have testified of being healed after hearing our teaching about evil spirits being the cause of many ailments. (You can watch our training videos at SpiritLifestyle.com).

OTHER HEALTH PROBLEMS

Undiagnosed conditions that for whatever reason seem to baffle medics often have a spiritual cause, such as fibromyalgia, which is simply a spirit of pain, or auto-immune diseases. Some conditions are more obviously caused by demons than others. Take OCD or Tourette's syndrome for example where the person acts involuntarily and cannot control their body's behavior or their bad language.

There are so many physical infirmities that can be directly caused by demons that I can't include them all here, but some other common ones include cancer, scoliosis (spirit of infirmity and crippling spirit), arthritis particularly rheumatoid or osteo arthritis (which is caused by a crippling spirit), other crippling diseases, wasting diseases, many hereditary conditions, strokes, heart attacks, migraines, chronic fatigue, ME, skin conditions, food intolerances and allergies, deafness and blindness, epilepsy. Not all these conditions are directly caused by demons, but very often in my experience of helping people get free and be healed, it has been a demon that is the cause.

Thankfully, if you have any of the above conditions or sense that you may have something else caused by a demon, you can get free simply and quickly. Through the power of Jesus, you can be healed and free in every area of your life and as you keep reading, you will find out how.

Not all illnesses are caused directly by demons. In my experience, migraine headaches do tend to have a spiritual cause but not always. At one of our events, I invited anyone to come up who had migraine headaches. When one woman was prayed for, the person praying could feel something like a finger sticking out of the woman's forehead poking their hand which they'd placed on her head! It was exactly where the woman said her head was hurting. They told it to leave and the pain moved to the other side. When they put their hand on that place, again they felt something like an invisible finger poking them. It was obvious this was a demon, and when it was told to leave by the woman receiving prayer, it left and all the pain went with it. So in that case, the migraines were caused by an evil spirit.

However, many moons ago during my twenties, I had

severe headaches on and off for about ten years. I didn't know then what I know now about healing and deliverance, but nothing would get rid of the pain and I would have to go and lie down for hours in the dark when the pain came. Eventually I decided to try cutting down on caffeine in my tea and since I did that I have not had a bad headache since! This goes to show that as well as looking after our spiritual health, we also need to take care of our bodies and live healthy lives with good food and plenty of exercise too.

CHAPTER FOUR

Mental Health And Freedom For The Soul

I n this chapter we're going to look at how the demonic manifests through our thought life and maladies of the mind. This is not to stigmatize mental illness, but to highlight the close relationship between the mind and the physical body and how evil spirits can monopolize our thought life to bring us further into the spiritual prisons of darkness.

We will identify some of the most prevalent mental health issues such as depression, self-harm and trauma and explore the spiritual root nature of these problems. Finally, we will outline the route to freedom and wellbeing through the act of deliverance.

According to many Bible teachers, our soul consists of our mind, our emotions and our will. My body and my soul are to be subject to my spirit and my spirit to be one with the Spirit of God (see Romans 8). The devil wants me to believe and live as though my soul and body have free reign but sadly, living that way leads to corruption, torment, slavery and death. If my body and soul are subject to my spirit which is one with the Spirit of God, this brings life, purity, freedom and light.

MENTAL HEALTH

Despite often being a result of past trauma, many mental health issues actually have a spiritual root. Discovering the spiritual power behind conditions such as depression, bi-polar, self-harm, confusion, imaginary friends, OCD, ADD, autism, schizophrenia, phobias, anxieties and various disorders can help bring swift and permanent freedom.

I was speaking to a large crowd one time and the Holy Spirit showed me that a person in that meeting had witnessed something horrific in their past, like a violent death and suffered from ongoing trauma as a result. A vision flashed before my eyes of a lot of blood and an awful incident which I went on to describe. A young woman raised her hand and told us all how as a girl she had witnessed an horrific murder right in front of her. Her life had been dramatically impacted as a result to such a degree that she suffered terribly from the trauma in many ways.

After releasing the peace of Jesus into her life, we told

the spirit of trauma to leave her. It left with some force and she fell backwards some distance onto the floor. She was unhurt, but when she got up, she knew all the trauma had left her. We saw her again a year or so later and she told us that she had been completely set free from that demon and her life had been transformed as a result. Years of medication and counselling were unable to help her, but she was instantly freed through the power of Jesus.

Our Miracle Cafés attract a lot of people. Not just for the good food and drinks, but many are also drawn to our free spiritual menu. Freedom from negative thoughts and anxiety is a popular request from our customers. And it's no wonder, with pandemics, wars, unrest, economies and the like being in turbulence, not to mention ill health, loss, financial and relationship issues.

In another chapter we will talk more about a spirit of anxiety and fear, but suffice to say here, whenever we come into agreement in any way with an evil spirit and give it a place in our life, we empower it. We must break agreement and stop its influence in order to live free.

"Refuse to worry about tomorrow but deal with each challenge that comes your way, one day at a time. Tomorrow will take care of itself" (Matthew 6:34 TPT).

FREEDOM FROM MENTAL TORMENT AND PAIN

There are many ways that people try to release their inner pain and gain mental and emotional freedom; not all are helpful. Alcohol, drugs, over-eating, casual sex, gambling and so on may seem to bring short term relief, but only exacerbate the problem with feelings of guilt and shame, causing an even further spiralling downwards. Another outlet that seems to be popular, particularly amongst younger people is that of self-harm.

WHAT IS SELF-HARM AND WHY DO PEOPLE DO IT?

According to the mental health organisation Mind, self-harm is "when you hurt yourself as a way of dealing with very difficult feelings, painful memories or overwhelming situations and experiences".

These are some of the reasons people self-harm:

- to express something that is hard to put into words
- turn invisible thoughts or feelings into something visible
- change emotional pain into physical pain
- reduce overwhelming emotional feelings or thoughts
- have a sense of being in control
- escape traumatic memories

- have something in life that they can rely on
- punishment for feelings and experiences
- stop feeling numb, disconnected or dissociated
- create a reason to physically care for oneself
- express suicidal feelings and thoughts without taking one's own life.

CASES OF SELF-HARM ARE ON THE INCREASE

The number of young people arriving in hospital emergency after self-harming or taking overdoses is not only much greater since the start of the Covid-19 pandemic, but the number of younger children self-harming is also increasing, reports Dr John Wright of Bradford Royal Infirmary Hospital.

According to the National Library of Medicine, an international survey taken in 2015 concluded that:

- About 17% of all people self-harm during their lifetime
- The average age of the first incident of self-harm is 13
- About 50% of people seek help for self-harming (mainly from friends)

Feelings of hopelessness, despair, rejection, torment and failure often accompany acts of self-harm along with a sense of guilt and inadequacy.

One of the problems of self-harming is that even though a short-term feeling of release is felt, the underlying cause of the problem is not dealt with, and the self-harmer can begin a vicious (quite literally) circle, similar to an addiction, that is difficult to break. Not to mention the physical pain, mutilation and scars that result.

ONE YOUNG WOMAN'S EXPERIENCE

Noemi, a young woman from Madrid was abused by a close family member as a child. After later confronting her abuser, she was accused of lying and told she was evil. Noemi explained to me recently, that as a result of what had happened: "My mind was so negative. I felt so much hatred towards him, I was absolutely full of hate. The abuse affected many areas of my life and it was horrible. As a teenager I was so rebellious. My heart became hardened towards people. There are many ways you can harm yourself through food, sex, bad relationships, cutting yourself and I did most of them! I remember when I was thirteen, I would make myself vomit because I didn't like the way I was."

In a moment we'll look at how Noemi got free and what dramatically transformed her life for the better. But first, let's look at current treatments that are often employed.

COMMON TREATMENTS FOR SELF-HARM

There are several different methods that can be used to treat self-harm, which concentrate on either treating the underlying causes or on treating the behavior itself. Other approaches involve avoidance techniques, which focus on keeping the individual occupied with other activities, or replacing the act of self-harm with safer methods that do not lead to permanent damage.

Common treatments for self-harm may go some way to alleviate the problem, but the best way is to address the root cause.

WHAT DOCTORS DON'T TELL YOU

A little known fact is that the root cause of self-harm and many other emotional and mental health issues, is in fact spiritual. There are forces of darkness at play, and just because we don't often see them with our physical eyes, it doesn't mean they don't exist.

Let's hear more from Noemi: "As I was growing up, I thought that forgiving the person who abused me would help, but I couldn't forgive him, even though I tried. It was like a wall in front of me. But one day I asked the Holy Spirit to show me what it was and I saw that it was an evil spirit – the spirit of rejection – which caused me to feel rejected. I had been experiencing a horrible demon of self-harm. The spirit appeared to be in the form of a mirror that was distorted and each time I looked in it, it made me appear deformed." So, due to an evil spirit of rejection, Noemi wasn't seeing her true identity. The way she viewed herself was distorted.

Noemi goes on to say, "That mirror didn't show a true reflection of who I really was. Thankfully, I was delivered of that spirit. Once I saw the truth of what it was, I told the spirit to leave me at the name of Jesus and it went. Jesus has set me free and my heart is now merciful and sweet, my life has changed and I have been able to forgive." Noemi went on to become one of our Spirit Lifestyle Coaches in Spain, helping other people find hope, healing and freedom.

DARK FORCES AT WORK

According to the Bible, Jesus said, "The thief comes to steal, to kill and to destroy, but I have come that they may have life to the full" (John 10:10). The thief that Jesus is referring to here is Satan - the devil, and he works through evil spirits which in turn tend to work through people.

When bad things happen to us, evil spirits are often involved and because Satan is jealous of us and God's love for us, he tries to destroy our lives. As other people or circumstances come against us in life, it's important that we choose not to react in a way that would allow evil spirits to gain a foothold. How they do this is by causing us to feel anger, hatred, rejection, pain, confusion, self-pity, bitterness and so on. They often put thoughts into our minds that seem to be our own thoughts, but are actually lies or half-truths and we believe them.

The more we come into agreement with these thoughts and feelings, the more we will begin to spiral downwards into inner turmoil, depression, anxiety, self-loathing and other negative feelings which then lead to negative patterns of behavior.

In order to free ourselves from these dark thoughts and feelings, we look for a way out, a way to stop that happening. And if we don't recognize that the root cause of our problems is a result of our own poor choices or responses that have impacted us spiritually, and don't deal with that through the power of Jesus, then we will often turn to other outlets. Substance abuse, (alcohol, drugs etc), over-working, excessive exercise, eating disorders, shutting ourselves away from others, or self-harming in some other way such as inflicting pain on ourselves, are some of the ways we may do this.

Once free from the spirit of depression or addiction or whatever it is, then it's important to make the right choices each day and change our behavior. Repentance means to change the way we think and act.

SELF-HARM HELP AND FREEDOM

The way to freedom is simple. Once we recognize that the source of the problem is demonic, half the battle is won! In fact, the battle has already been won, because of what Jesus accomplished on the cross. Once the schemes of the enemy are exposed, it's simply a matter of submitting to Jesus and acknowledging that through Jesus' death on the cross and subsequent resurrection, the powers of darkness have been broken.

"Since the children have flesh and blood, He (Jesus) also shared in their humanity, so that by His death, He might break the power of him who holds the power of death – that is, the devil, and free those who all their lives were held in slavery…" (Hebrews 2:14).

The devil has been stripped of his legal right to enshroud us with death and all that comes with it!

This means that you no longer need to be subject to the power of Satan in your life. You can be free, right now! The gospel means 'good news' and this really is good news and it's true. Even as you read this truth, you may already start feeling lighter and more hopeful. That's the power of Jesus beginning to work in your life.

Noemi says, "Don't live according to the pain or the rebellious feelings inside because you will harm yourself even more and make things worse. So stop, go to Father God and allow Him to hug you and speak to you. Nothing compares with that." We would also advise anyone self-harming or with suicidal thoughts to share their struggles with an encouraging person they can trust who is able to help walk with them on their path to freedom.

SUPERNATURAL SCAR REMOVAL

Alexandria, one of our Spirit Lifestyle team members, shares this amazing true story about something that happened in her Idaho Café:

"One day, a young gentleman around 23 years of age poked his head around the door and asked if he could just sit in our café because he said it felt good in there. I explained it was probably the presence of Jesus he could feel. He seemed happy about that and told me he'd just given his life to Jesus – apparently he'd been involved in the occult previously. I hadn't seen him before, but I began to share God's heart for him and God's destiny for him and his identity that the Holy Spirit showed me. The young guy was delighted and surprised that I knew things about him, even though we hadn't met before.

As I continued to pray blessings over him, his eyes

started to get big and it was weird as he kept looking at his arms. He could hardly contain himself as he pulled back his sleeves. 'Look, look, look!' he said. We watched and could see scars from self-harming on both his arms – it was almost as though the finger of God moved across his arms and erased the scars as we watched them disappear. We watched as miracles broke out right there for that young guy as God erased the scars of self-harm."

I love this true story and it shows that God not only loves to heal the emotional and mental wounds and scars, but also physical scars too. It happened as this young man began to get the revelation of God's love for him and his true identity and destiny in Jesus. It's interesting that Noemi also got free when the evil spirit was revealed as a distorted mirror and she was then able to discover her true identity in God.

DON'T GIVE A PLACE FOR HOPELESSNESS

The enemy accuses us, and seeks to wear us out and beat us down: "Just quit – no-one's going to help you." He causes us to fear the worst, to be tormented by anxiety and negative thoughts and difficult circumstances. It's like he's trying to besiege us and surround us on every side so we surrender and eventually just give up.

But this is not a time to be besieged and to be

constantly fighting the enemy. God has given us our 'Promised Land' which the book of Hebrews describes as a place of rest. However, when the Israelites entered their Promised Land, even though it was a land 'flowing with milk and honey' they still had to fight the inhabitants of the land that had unrightfully been living there. They had to drive them out. It's time to completely change our thinking. Instead of feeling 'under attack' which is a distraction from the enemy, our place is to be on the offensive. We are in a spiritual battle to take ground that is rightfully ours, part of our inheritance, but we do this from a place of rest, secure in God.

Listen to this truth from Psalm 91:

"When you abide under the shadow of Shaddai (God the destroyer of enemies) you are hidden in the strength of God Most High. He's the hope that holds me and the stronghold to shelter me, the only God for me, and my great confidence. He will rescue you from every hidden trap of the enemy, and He will protect you from false accusation and any deadly curse. His massive arms are wrapped around you, protecting you. You can run under His covering of majesty and hide. His arms of faithfulness are a shield keeping you from harm. You will never worry about an attack of demonic forces at night nor have to fear a spirit of darkness coming against you.

Don't fear a thing... How then could evil prevail against us or disease infect us? God sends angels with special orders to protect you wherever you go, defending you from all harm" (from Psalm 91 TPT).

WHAT IS BEHIND DEPRESSION?

Depression can very often be caused by demons. Once, when I was relaxing in the garden on a lovely summer's day, a dark feeling came over me for no apparent reason. I began to feel sad and then depressed quite quickly. I was starting to take on board the depressing thoughts and felt very low, but instantly I realized these were not my thoughts and that I must not take them on board or agree with them. I recognized that a spirit of depression or despair (like that mentioned in Isaiah 61:3) had tried to settle on me, so I spoke out loud and commanded the spirit to leave in the name of Jesus. Immediately the feelings disappeared, and I was back to normal. I was shocked to realize that if I'd taken those thoughts any further and come into agreement with that demon, before long I could be suffering from depression. I think this happens to many people without them knowing it.

Demons torture, they enslave, they defile, they deceive, they cause addictions, they attack the physical body and the mind, they compel, they harass, they entice.

But to reiterate what we stated earlier, **"The mind**

governed by the Spirit is life and peace" (Romans 8:6). That is our true identity and inheritance, and it is up to us to choose this way of life each day.

EMOTIONAL FREEDOM

Isaiah 61 cites a spirit of despair which can also be translated 'heaviness'. Many people relate to a feeling of hopelessness, or despair as being a heavy feeling or a dark cloud upon them. They find it difficult to get up in the morning or to exercise, or even to go about the day's basic necessities of life.

Often this is a result of being betrayed or abandoned, even from a young age, or perhaps a traumatic experience, or sustained difficulties, or loss in life, or simply a lack of purpose.

If we allow feelings of rejection, hopelessness, anger, rebellion, hatred, bitterness, fear (and any negative emotion you can think of) to have a place in our life, then before long, evil spirits of rejection, hopelessness, anger, rebellion, hatred, bitterness, fear and so on, will take up residence in our emotions which is part of our soul. The result of this is that we become an angry person, or a fearful person or whatever, and those traits will manifest in our lives, no matter how hard we try to stop them.

The solution is to recognize the demons and get rid of

them and to go back to the root cause of those feelings – what caused that response in me in the first place? That needs to be dealt with and repentance is also necessary, which means changing the way we think and acting differently.

In a later chapter we'll put that into practice. For now, I'm helping you by bringing light into your life to reveal the dark places, and very soon that darkness will be leaving. When the light comes, the darkness must go.

Some of the most common emotional problems that are caused or exacerbated by demons are fear, resentment and rejection (feeling unwanted and unloved). There is also self-pity, jealousy, worry and insecurity. Add to these hatred, anger, jealousy, lack of self-worth, anxiety, and feeling hopeless, and there are the very common feelings of guilt, failure and pride. Many also experience terrible extended grief, inexplicable suicidal or murderous thoughts, and the list goes on!

Thoughts of revenge are usually from the enemy and lead to becoming 'overcome by evil'. I have heard from a number of Satanists who went down that route because they wanted to get revenge on someone who had hurt them. The Bible has wisdom on this: **"Do not repay anyone evil for evil. Be careful to do what is right in the eyes of everyone. If it is possible, as far** as it depends on you, live at peace with everyone. Do not take revenge, my dear friends, but leave room for God's wrath, for it is written: "It is mine to avenge; I will repay," says the Lord. On the contrary: If your enemy is hungry, feed him; if he is thirsty, give him something to drink. In doing this, you will heap burning coals on his head. Do not be overcome by evil, but overcome evil with good" (Romans 12:17-21).

"Resist revenge, and make sure that no one pays back evil in place of evil but always pursue doing what is beautiful to one another and to all the unbelievers" (1 Thessalonians 5:15 TPT).

Negative emotional patterns are likely to have a demonic connection and until that is addressed, the root cause cannot be dealt with.

It can be freeing to open up about emotions and to share feelings with others, but it can be a mistake to speak about it often or to focus on emotional pain or to carry a victim mentality. This can invite evil spirits to come in like flies to a festering wound. One of Satan's names, Beelzebub, actually means 'lord of the flies'. However, sharing feelings directly with God and bearing our soul to Him can enable Him to heal our heart if we are willing to allow Him in. You can tell Him of your hurts and emotional pain. He wants to heal you and set you free.

If we bottle up our emotional pain it will often lead to sickness, bitterness and a miserable existence, but if we choose to allow God to shine His light into our hearts and flood us with His glorious Spirit, then His love will heal us. So let's decide now to stop voicing the pain we feel to those we meet, and instead receive God's freedom, joy and peace where there was brokenness, pain and torment.

Perhaps pray this along with the Psalmist:

"God, I invite your searching gaze into my heart.
Examine me through and through;
find out everything that may be hidden within me.
Put me to the test and sift through all my anxious cares.
See if there is any path of pain I'm walking on,
and lead me back to your glorious, everlasting way—
the path that brings me back to you"
(Psalm 139:23-24 TPT).

A SNIPER ON MY DOORSTEP

A sniper knocked on my door. Well, actually he used to be a sniper in the British Army but now he's a delivery man. He remarked on the stunning location of the Welsh cottage we were in and asked how we ended up living there. I told him how the Holy Spirit had got us to pack up our home, to get in the car and follow wherever He led us, and that was where we'd ended up temporarily. I shared how after we'd arrived I read an old journal entry where years back, I'd written the dreams of my heart, and how what we were doing and where we were staying was exact in almost every detail to what I'd had in my heart. And that by being obedient to the Lord's call, He'd miraculously brought us there.

Without knowing anything about the man, I began to prophesy and the Lord showed me how He'd kept him safe and preserved his life over the years and that He'd been chosen by God and now it was time to follow Jesus.

The delivery man was amazed and shared with me how he'd been a sniper. He had to admit that he'd been close to death so many times, and perhaps it was God who had protected him. At the time, he couldn't fathom why he was still alive.

POST-TRAUMATIC STRESS DISORDER

However, after being posted to war zones throughout the 1980s and 90s he told me that he still had PTSD after all those years and how it had caused him and his wife to split up. He got to such a low point that he tried to kill himself – he told me the steps he took to end his life, but at the last minute his dog licked his hand which caused him not to go through with it.

I don't think he had a relationship with God, but he bravely told me how he'd cried through the night and begged God to help him. Amazingly he explained how after crying out to God, he and his wife got back together, but still, even now, he was unable to sleep. Not only did he constantly have awful flashbacks where he saw horrific images, but he regularly smelled the putrid stench from war, even after all those years.

My heart went out to him and he let me pray. Keeping the required two metre distance during the Covid lockdown, I stretched out my hand and he put his over his heart. I could sense the power of God touching him and I released the love of the Father into his body, soul and spirit, to cleanse him of all bad memories and of trauma. I gave him one of my booklets 'Your Spirit Life' and I wrote down our friend's name, 'Neil Obbard', for him to check out; he was also a sniper in the Army and had come to faith. As well as writing a book on his own life, Neil's incredible story also features in my book, 'Unexpected Miracles'.

A SECOND VISIT

A few weeks later, the ex-sniper was back delivering our groceries again. He told me how since the day I prayed for him on my doorstep, he slept soundly all night, every night. He used to violently levitate up from the bed while he was sleeping because of the torment, and it would disturb his wife. But since I asked the Lord to cleanse the bad memories and the trauma, he now sleeps well. He told me it had been 15 years since he last slept properly. But now he feels peace and that everything is well with him. I could have hugged him but managed to remain at a distance! God is so good.

YOU TOO CAN BE FREE!

The power of Jesus is available today to set you and your loved ones free forever. Just call on His name and receive it by faith. Let Jesus into your mind, your heart, into your spirit, soul and body and be healed, set free from trauma, from torment, from any thoughts of ending your life. Let the Holy Spirit wash away all painful and negative memories in the name of Jesus and receive His peace and life everlasting. God loves you and you can be free, right now, through the power of Jesus!

CHAPTER FIVE

Spiritual Freedom

Involvement in false religions, including New Age practices, can open a door for demons to enter. If we have been involved in any religion (even Christian if it places religious activity over a relationship with Jesus) then we can unwittingly open a door to evil spirits.

Buddhism, Hinduism, Islam, Baha'i, Eastern philosophies or any practice related to Eastern religions such as Yoga, Reiki and even Karate – anything with a spiritual power or 'energy' that is not the Holy Spirit, can open us up to evil spirits.

Cults, even so-called 'Christian' ones such as Mormonism, Jehovah's Witness and Christian Science deny some of the fundamental teachings of Scripture and can open participants up to demonic spirits.

There is a 'religious' spirit that often goes unnoticed

by the person influenced by it, no matter what denomination or stream of Christianity they are in. Someone can think they are a Christian, however, they are not in a loving relationship with God, but act out of religious duty. They are often judgmental and critical of others who are full of the Holy Spirit. The Pharisees in Jesus' day epitomized a religious spirit. They missed what God was doing and ultimately were the ones who called for Jesus to be crucified and incited others to condemn Him to death.

RELIGIOUS SPIRIT

If you have been brought up in 'religion' or some kind of cult or got side-tracked from your walk with Jesus into having to attain your salvation by doing good works, or spend your time trying not to do 'bad' things, then you may have picked up a spirit of religion along the way. Very often this demon manifests by fault-finding, by accusing others, being critical, judgmental, controlling and manipulating. The spirit of racism also comes under this category. We can be freed from this, but, as with most demonic influence, we will need to change our behavior and thought processes pretty dramatically. This, however, should come as a result of our love for Jesus and God's grace in our lives, not by 'trying' to do it in our own strength.

Let's hear from a young lady who grew up in an

abusive religious household and how she got free. Please note - not all religious families are like this. Any person or household can be abusive without being religious, but this woman's experience is not uncommon.

"I was raised in a strict religious household and my family was highly dysfunctional. My father was a violent alcoholic and so I didn't have much of a childhood. A lot of horrific things happened. My father would threaten me with knives and he beat my mother for years. Every week I would be dragged out of bed by my hair, beaten and forced to go to the temple with my family.

I left home when my dad was having a psychotic alcoholic episode, breaking my door down and trying to kill me. Then three months after I left home I was raped. I went into a world of my own for ten months and relied heavily on alcohol, then had a nervous breakdown. My mother then had a brain haemorrhage followed by a stroke and my whole family went into meltdown and fell out with each other. That same year I had a car accident where I nearly died and my lounge ceiling fell in and my bathroom had to be refitted three times. I came to the end of myself and had a lot of fear.

One time, when I was in semi-sleep I saw an amazing white light. I woke up and said, 'God if you're real, you have to come right now. If you can remove the pain from my life then I will serve you for the rest of my days.' I began to feel an amazing energy begin to circle my entire body. It was the power of God and felt really powerful, scarily powerful. That was how Jesus came into my life. Now I love Jesus with all my heart and soul, every ounce of my being."

This young lady came to a workshop we hosted on deliverance from demons. I'd shared some teaching and then asked people to get into groups of three and pray for each other. She described what happened to her. "I had come to the workshop because I wanted to learn more. A small group of people prayed for me and I fell to the floor. There seemed to be a real heaviness on my chest going through to my stomach. It was very black and it was holding onto me. It began to make its way all the way up within me and I was just screaming. I didn't even recognize my own voice. That big black thing released from my body. It was the demons coming out, there were another four or five that came out of my body. One of the other workshop attendees could hear demonic screams in the spirit realm a few minutes before they came out of me."

Months later, she explained, "I now feel a lot lighter and more connected to God. Some of the fears I had, have now completely gone. I feel spiritually refreshed and ready to serve God more than ever before. My friends and family have commented that there is a marked difference in me since I came to that workshop.

It's absolutely astounding, it's been life-changing for me and I'm so excited. God is so fantastic, I love Jesus!"

BREAKING THE POWER OF THE OCCULT

An obvious door of entry to demons is involvement in the occult which includes Paganism, Witchcraft, Satanism and the like. What many do not realize is that Freemasonry and Spiritism also fall into this category. Magic (not simply card tricks but the type that uses spiritual power and often illusionists), ouija boards, seances, fortune telling, automatic handwriting, levitation, astral projection, palmistry, horoscopes, hypnosis, ESP, astrology, divination, tarot and such like are all part of the occult. The Bible is clear that any form of seeking supernatural knowledge, guidance and power apart from the Spirit of Jesus - the Holy Spirit, is dangerous (see Deuteronomy 18:9-15).

THE DANGERS OF DIVINATION

Luke's account of the Apostle Paul's encounter with a fortune teller is interesting: **"Once when we were going to the place of prayer, we were met by a female slave who had a spirit (demon) by which she predicted the future. She earned a great deal of money for her owners by fortune-telling. She followed Paul and the rest of us, shouting, "These men are servants of the Most High God, who are telling you the way to be saved." She kept this up for**

many days. Finally Paul became so annoyed that he turned around and said to the spirit, "In the name of Jesus Christ I command you to come out of her!" At that moment the spirit left her" (Acts 16:16-18).

Here the slave girl was speaking words which were true, but those words did not come from the Holy Spirit, they came from a demon. This goes to show that fortune-tellers, mediums and the like, may seem to know information, but often the spirit that is supplying them the information is in fact a demon. And since the devil has an assignment against us to steal, kill and destroy, it's unwise to put ourselves in situations where that could happen. Thankfully it is simple to come out from under that destructive assignment when we recognize what is at work spiritually and ask God to forgive us. Keep reading and I will help you do this in an upcoming chapter.

The Word of God is clear that Jesus is the only safe and legal access point into the realm of the spirit (see John 10:9). If we are involved in any sort of spiritual practice or belief outside of Jesus, we are likely to attract demonic spirits.

"When someone tells you to consult mediums and spiritists, who whisper and mutter... Then they will look toward the earth and see only distress and darkness and fearful gloom, and they will be thrust into utter darkness" (Isaiah 8:19).

BLACK WITCHCRAFT AND SATANISM

I interviewed Debra for my book 'Unexpected Miracles' and here she describes how she became entangled in the occult:

"I became a 'White Witch' in the 1990s and was part of several covens. I was involved as a witch for a number of years and I was also drawn into Druidism, Hinduism, Buddhism, New Age and Theosophy, but my life always seemed to be a struggle. One day, my partner attacked me and a friend with a knife. It was such an horrific thing to happen to me that after the incident, I began to suffer from post-traumatic stress. Nothing I tried could help my state of mind.

I felt completely powerless from the knife attack and wanted something in my life that would help empower me. I bought books on voodoo and began to cast spells using voodoo, then delved into black witchcraft and satanism. I ended up making a pact with the devil and as I did this, demons entered and began tormenting me. I was enticed into buying more and more books to study, but ironically, the more power I searched for, the less I was in control and the more the demons had power over me. I would hear voices in my head telling me what to do and I knew I was coming under a dark influence, but I didn't know how to stop.

As I continued in the occult, demons would speak loudly in my head and order me to do things. I was under the influence and control of demons and I needed a way out. Desperately, I prayed to God: "This isn't right, what can I do!?" Soon after this, on Good Friday, I had a vision of Jesus and He told me to take all the demonic books and have them burned. I did this on Easter Sunday. Then I asked Jesus to come into my life and one week later I was baptized in the sea off the North Wales coast, near my home.

Jesus spoke to me. He was full of love and I felt peace and clarity when He spoke. He led me to watch a TV program with Aliss. She was talking about Jesus and her relationship with the Holy Spirit and she seemed to move in power unlike anything I'd come across before. But it was a pure power, full of God's love. She seemed happy and I knew I needed a relationship with God like she had. I then read all her books and that was when I started really connecting to Jesus. I also booked myself onto a conference which Rob and Aliss were organizing.

No-one knew me, but as Aliss stood at the front of the meeting, I felt Jesus come up to me in a huge bright white light. Looking straight at me, Aliss called out, "There's somebody here who's just given their life to Jesus and has been reading my books." I was shocked but went up onto the stage and shared some of my story with her in front of hundreds of people.

Everyone there stretched out their hands and began to pray over me as I went back to my seat.

I was aware of an incredible figure in front of me. It was Jesus and He was wearing robes that were so white and emanated a brilliant white light. He began to pull things out of the top of my head. I could feel demons being pulled out. I'd been in a lot of pain with my back and shoulders and throughout my body and then I realized I was totally and utterly pain free and I just felt amazing. After that, I felt the presence of Jesus so strong like He was standing right next to me and I could feel His robe brushing against me.

Following my encounter with Jesus at the conference, not only was I pain free, but I also no longer needed the antidepressant medication I had been taking. Up until the conference I practiced and taught Reiki, but afterwards discovered I could no longer do it. I gave up teaching it immediately; the Lord had totally removed it from me, and instead I was releasing the healing power of Jesus.

I told all the demons to leave me and they did, as soon as I broke any agreement with them, and my skin condition left too.

A few years ago, I changed my name to a demonic name, to try and get more power. But when I gave my life to Jesus, I knew I needed to get rid of that name, so

I changed it back to the name I was given as a baby. It wasn't easy to change as all my friends were using my demonic name but doing that brought freedom too.

I know that the power of Jesus works. I can see it works. It has worked in my life. I know God is real. Jesus is the highest power, far greater than any demonic power. What I feel now is pure; I'm tuning into a different energy totally, it's the power of Jesus, the Holy Spirit. Following Jesus is incredible. I no longer feel powerless. As I lay down my life, He lives through me and He is so powerful.

Going through the experience that I did has made it clear to me that the devil is real, that demons are real and they work through what we sometimes perceive as 'good', even 'white witchcraft'. But I don't even have to think about the bad stuff from my past since I gave my life to Jesus as it's gone. I went through some dreadful things in my life, particularly with the stabbing, but the physical and emotional pain doesn't exist anymore: I'm free."

THE DANGERS OF WICCA

While writing this book, I've been asking the Holy Spirit to make it clear to me what to write and what to leave out, as I have so many stories I could share. I had a dream last night and saw large letters landing in front of me W-I-C-C-A and then I woke up and knew I needed to write about Wicca as it would help someone reading this to get free.

Wicca, a type of witchcraft, involves the worship of nature and using spiritual forces to get results. It seems to be a fast growing 'religion' amongst young girls, popularized by recent TV shows, books and movies. Magic and spellcasting are an integral part of Wicca. Wiccans say that spells are symbolic acts performed in an altered state of consciousness to cause a desired change. There are spells to attract money, increase power, cause harm to others, attract love and so on.

But the dangers of being involved in any type of occult practice are many. If we cast spells (even so-called good ones), read tarot cards, play with Ouija boards, visit a medium or even have our fortune read, then we are likely to have attracted demons into our life. Not only do I advise stopping those practices, but by continuing to read this book and praying along with the prayers, you will learn the truth and can be set free completely.

The occult means 'hidden' or 'darkness' and anything done in secret darkness is now being exposed by the light of Jesus. Secret societies, even those that pertain to be charitable, such as Freemasonry, use secretive, occultic rituals.

I believe there is someone reading this right now who has been involved in the occult or some kind of secret darkness and is about to get free. In fact, evil spirits are beginning to leave without you even praying, just by simply reading this and allowing the Light to come into your heart.

FREEDOM FROM WITCHCRAFT

We were hosting a workshop in South Carolina, and during the introductions, a couple sitting on the front row told us they had come all the way from Texas because they wanted to give their lives to Jesus. So they, along with their sister who had come from Central America, prayed and asked Jesus into their lives. Later they explained that a witch had put a curse and voodoo spells on them and for two years they had been living in torment. They couldn't sleep, they'd got the police involved but there was nothing they could do. The couple told us how they had no life; they were scared for themselves and their children, and always looking over their shoulders.

They knew they were powerless to break the witchcraft and even considered moving to another city. But they saw me sharing about the power of Jesus on TV and discovered that He has the power to set them free. After that workshop when they surrendered their lives to Jesus, they told us everything changed.

94

Three weeks after we first met at the workshop, they received an email from the witch saying she was so sorry for all the trouble she'd caused them; all the problems ceased, and the witch even told them that she needed Jesus too!

A few months later when we were hosting another workshop, this time in Texas, the couple came to the front to share their amazing story. The rest of their family including their children and father asked Jesus into their lives too. Submitting our lives to Jesus is powerful. His blood breaks the power of Satan, including witchcraft.

THE PRICE OF REBELLION

It is not only witches that are involved in witchcraft; did you know that our prayers can be witchcraft too? The Bible says that rebellion is as the sin of witchcraft (1 Samuel 15:23). If we go outside of God's plan and try to make things happen in the way that we pray, or by declaring or proclaiming our will instead of God's, we can open ourselves up to evil spirits. It is so important to pray in accordance with God's will. Jesus said He only did and spoke what He saw the Father doing in heaven. Let's be inspired to live the same way (see John 5:19).

When God's people in the Old Testament were too full of fear to go in and take the land God had promised them, Joshua urged them not to rebel against God. Only two out of the whole nation went on to inherit what was promised. The rest of that generation died in the wilderness. Let us learn from this: before God's promises can be fulfilled in our lives, we must step out in faith, face our fears head on, and trust that God is able to do what He has promised. If we give in to fear or other distractions from the enemy, then we will not inherit our promises either, and will be in rebellion to God.

There is hope for us though, even if we have been in rebellion in the past. Isaiah the prophet foretold of the coming Jesus and the incredible sacrifice He would make for us: **"We all, like sheep, have gone astray, each of us has turned to our own way (rebelled); and the Lord has laid on Him the iniquity of us all" (Isaiah 53:6).**

Going our own way is rebellion. The original Hebrew word there in the text means 'rebellion and all evil consequences of rebellion and guilt.' Jesus took our guilt and rebellion and paid the ultimate price when He died on the cross so that we can be set free from all the evil consequences. But in order to live free we must continue to make right choices and remain surrendered to the resurrected Jesus.

THE DANGEROUS PRACTICE OF MANIFESTING

'Manifesting' is a term often used by Christians to describe outward spiritual activity in a person whether through the Holy Spirit or through demons, but recently it has also become a name for the popular craze that is growing, particularly amongst young people.

On social media there are millions of followers of those who teach others to 'manifest' whatever they want. The idea is to set yourself a goal and then to 'will' it to happen by spiritual means. Typically the goals are to become rich and successful, achieve top results in exams, attract a particular person, own an expensive car, be popular, be attractive, get ahead at work, and so on.

According to a recent BBC news article, "Manifesting comes from New Thought philosophy, a 19th century spiritual movement from the United States that put an emphasis on spiritual healing and metaphysics. The philosophy's Law of Attraction theory - that positive or negative thoughts can bring positive or negative realities into a person's life - lies at the heart of manifesting, where believers are certain they can create their own realities with the right process."

#Manifesting has had 334mn views on TikTok - and #manifestation sits at a whopping 4.3bn" (stats from a

BBC article by S Galer, Sept 2020).

In many cases 'manifesting' does seem to work. However, what many don't realize, or maybe don't even care about, is the fact that this is witchcraft.

Witches use spells, incantations and control to force an outcome, and this is what is happening through the current trend in 'manifesting'. Involvement in any form of witchcraft opens a door in our lives to the demonic. Positive thinking on its own is not a bad thing; in fact most of us could probably benefit from thinking more positively. But the promises of God and the fullness of our inheritance in Christ are all available to us THROUGH FAITH IN JESUS (see Ephesians 2:8 and Hebrews 11) and by SURRENDERING OUR LIVES and our will to His - being obedient to Him, led by the Holy Spirit in all we do and say.

If we attempt to grasp what we want or think is right for us through any other means, whether simply through positive thinking or through 'manifesting' using witchcraft, control and manipulation, then we will find ourselves on a dark path. **"Enter through the narrow gate. For wide is the gate and broad is the road that leads to destruction, and many enter through it. But small is the gate and narrow the road that leads to life, and only a few find it" (Matthew 7:13,14).**

ONE GIRL'S JOURNEY INTO DARKNESS

Lisa explains: "It started when I was just seven years old. My best friend believed in unicorns and magicians. One day I said, "I really like your hair bobble" and she quite matter-of-factly replied that it came from a magician. She shared with me a sort of magical prayer which would make a hair bobble manifest from the magician. I went outside into the garden and put my hands out really expecting with all my faith for a hair bobble to materialize and it did, the following day. I got the hair bobbles I wanted, but I also unconsciously opened a door in my life to the occult, even as a seven-year-old."

In my book 'Unexpected Miracles' Lisa goes on to share the rest of her story of how she spent years being sucked further and further along that dark road until things came to a head one day in her occult business when the real Jesus walked in and confronted her after she had visited our shop in Chester! Since that day, her life has transformed. She now helps others encounter the light of Jesus, but for years she was living under the oppression of demons and warns of the dangers of manifesting and all other areas of the occult.

WILL THE REAL JESUS PLEASE STAND UP!

The Bible warns us about a counterfeit Jesus. Just as Eve was deceived in the beginning by Satan when he appeared as a serpent, we too can be deceived (see 2 Corinthians 11:3,4). In this present day and age, we come across various versions of Jesus: the New Age version which portrays an Eastern mystical 'Jesus' who mixes the gospel message of the Bible with the Eastern teachings and practices of Buddhism and Hinduism.

There is also a 'Jesus' whom the humanists and universalists speak of. He is full of love and forgiveness but makes no mention of sin, of the need for repentance or of hell. Then there is the materialistic message of 'Jesus'. He meets all our needs and gives us the best of worldly materialism. But never mentions holiness or laying down our life and carrying our cross or being one with Him in His suffering.

The Bible is clear: accept another 'Jesus', a counterfeit 'Jesus' and instead of receiving the Holy Spirit, you will receive a 'different spirit'; that is, one or more demons.

There is also a counterfeit spirit that masquerades as the Holy Spirit. I meet many people who are happy to talk about the Holy Spirit and say they feel the power of the Holy Spirit when practicing Reiki or other spiritual practices, but sadly they are mistaken. The Holy Spirit is God and we cannot have the Holy Spirit without Jesus. He is the Spirit of Jesus (Philippians 1:19, Acts 16:7). The Holy Spirit always leads people to Jesus. The counterfeit Holy Spirit can even deceive Christians and can feel or appear like the true Spirit of

God, so it is always important to 'test the spirits' and if you are unsure, simply tell any spirit that is contrary to the Holy Spirit to leave and invite the true Spirit of Jesus to be present tangibly and to speak to you. The best way is to get to know Him – He will never contradict the Bible or bring fear, torment or confusion.

"Beloved, do not believe every spirit, but test the spirits to see whether they are from God"
(1 John 4:1).

ANGELS OF LIGHT

Belief in angels is common. Angels are around us and those sent by God help us and bring us messages. However, if we are not following Jesus, then we have the potential to be deceived by evil spirits masquerading as angels (see 2 Corinthians 11:14). We need to use the 'gift of discerning spirits' we read about in 1 Corinthians 12.

Sensing an evil presence, having harmful thoughts or an uneasy feeling in the pit of your stomach are clear signs that the 'angel' appearing to you is from the enemy. However, an 'angel of light' can appear beautiful and want to guide you and appear 'good'. If in doubt, as a follower of Jesus you can speak out loud to the spirit and say something like, "Light of Jesus come and reveal what this spirit is. Any spirit that is contrary to the Holy Spirit and that is against God's purposes I tell you to leave in the name of Jesus."

Adrian was a Psychic Medium when we first met him. He did tarot card readings, practised Reiki healing and would stand in front of audiences, as 'spirit guides' gave him messages 'from the other side'. He had been a Medium for decades until the day he came into our Blacon café and met Jesus. Without anyone telling him, he shredded all his occult literature and his tarot cards. The last card he shredded was the devil holding puppets on strings and he felt he had been like one of those puppets; but not anymore!

He asked us to pray alongside him as he told the 'spirit guides' to leave at the name of Jesus. He watched these spirit guides as they changed appearance from attractive beings into what they really were - ugly demons, and then they left. He was filled with the Holy Spirit, we baptized him in water, and he went on to volunteer in our shop and become part of a local church leadership team. You can read Adrian's incredible story in my book, "Unexpected Miracles."

The more we get to know God, meditate on His word and experience His presence, the more we will be able to discern a demonic spirit. But just because demons sometimes appear to be 'angels' we must not be put off from expecting and interacting with the angels and messengers sent by God.

If unsure, ask the Holy Spirit. When I sense an angel, I often ask the Spirit of Jesus to show me the purpose of the angel. It is scriptural to speak with angels – many in the Bible did so - and we can simply ask any angel that we see or sense if they serve Jesus. Sometimes when I sense angelic presence, I will speak out loud and say something like, "I welcome every messenger sent by God, and if you have come in the name of Jesus and are here to help me then please do. If you have a message, I would love to hear it!" Then wait to hear what the angel has to say.

I did this one time when a wind came into the room and I sensed an angel appear. I asked Holy Spirit what it was and immediately thought of Daniel and the angel that came to him with a message. So I spoke to the angel and asked him to give me the message he was bringing from the Lord. I 'knew' that we were to leave our home and belongings and follow the Holy Spirit wherever He was leading us. The message was brought by an angel, we both prayed into it, received dramatic confirmation, and quickly knew it was God's direction for us. It's been quite an adventure as we set out on the journey that so far has resulted in opening Miracle Cafés and Spirit Lifestyle Classes in many nations.

But if the Holy Spirit had shown me it was a demonic spirit that had appeared to me, I would simply have told it to jog on!

These that I've mentioned are just some of the many doorways that evil spirits can use as access points into our lives. Hopefully you are not able to relate to each and every one, but even if you do, the good news is you can be free to live a wonderful life in right standing with God and - it is so simple. Keep reading and very soon I'll be helping you through the steps to freedom through Jesus. You may even be sensing some freedom already!

CHAPTER SIX

How Demons Can Affect Us Through Others

Demons often operate through people. Of course, they will seek to come against us directly by invading our lives, putting thoughts in our heads and working adversely in our hearts. But a lot of what they do is through others, particularly those we are close to; our family members, colleagues and those in authority over us.

It is imperative that we get the revelation of this truth: **"Our battle is not against flesh and blood but against the (spiritual) rulers and authorities and powers of this dark world and against the spiritual forces of evil in the heavenly realms" (Ephesians 6:12).**

Let's apply this truth to various scenarios and really begin to uncover some of the ways in which the enemy works.

OUR RELATIONSHIPS

A couple told us that although their marriage was good on the whole, they had reached a crisis and a stalemate, and they were on the brink of separation. The husband had become secretive in areas of his life and from time to time, negative behaviors had surfaced which caused the wife to question what he was doing and find fault in many of his actions.

This fault-finding and accusation from the wife caused the husband to retreat further and to become angry and resentful towards his wife. The Holy Spirit showed us that the husband had unwittingly opened a door to demons of addiction and rebellion during his teenage years and the wife, trying to control his behavior so she wasn't hurt again, had come into agreement with demons of control, manipulation, fault finding and accusation.

When the Lord brought this light into the situation, the wife agreed and said that she would physically begin to shake when she was accusing or questioning him and now recognized that as being a manifestation of the demon. The demons on both sides were clashing and causing the wedge between husband and wife to increase until it looked as though their marriage may end.

2 Corinthians 10:4-6 TPT is pertinent here: **"For**

although we live in the natural realm, we don't wage a military campaign employing human weapons, using manipulation to achieve our aims. Instead, our spiritual weapons are energized with divine power to effectively dismantle the defences behind which people hide. We can demolish every deceptive fantasy that opposes God and break through every arrogant attitude that is raised up in defiance of the true knowledge of God. We capture, like prisoners of war, every thought and insist that it bow in obedience to the Anointed One. Since we are armed with such dynamic weaponry, we stand ready to punish any trace of rebellion as soon as you choose complete obedience."

Thankfully, when both the husband and wife understood what was going on spiritually and how the enemy was trying to split them up, the resolution came quickly. The husband confessed his sin of rebellion and addiction and poor choices, and the wife confessed her sin of accusation, fault finding, control and manipulation. After repentance and many tears and hugs, both husband and wife got free from those evil spirits, they changed their behavior and are now closer than ever with a very happy marriage!

Similarly, we've come across other situations such as a controlling parent and rebellious child, an angry husband or boss and a wife or employee full of anxiety, lack of self-worth and feelings of rejection.

Again, demons are at play on both sides.

If you have a difficult relationship, ask the Holy Spirit to come into the situation and bring light and revelation. We have seen many miracles happen when both parties recognize evil spirits at work, identify what they are, and be humble enough to admit coming into agreement with them. Then it's simply a matter of confessing, repenting, getting rid of those demons and coming together as a powerful force against the spiritual powers that are wanting to destroy your relationship.

Do this and follow the way of love, instead of battling one another and you will find freedom comes easily. Even if the other person is not willing to recognize spiritual forces at work, at least if you can be free and demonstrate love in all your dealings with them, God can work with that, and your love will have an impact.

"The Lord is near to those who have a broken heart, and saves those who have a contrite spirit" (Psalm 34:18).

As I write this, there are some crazy court cases going on where celebrities are wanting to prove they are right – today I read of one between two women who were best friends and the other between a divorced couple. In both cases, each party is suing the other for something they did or did not say or do and they have both turned into slanging matches, not for money, but to prove they are 'right'.

If we want to stay free from evil spirits, we need to give up our 'right to be right' and let it go. Forgive one another as we have been forgiven. Don't feel you always have to have the last say. This happens so much in relationships and is often the cause of division. Choose not to play into the devil's hand in this way.

FEAR MASQUERADING AS WISDOM

Satan often uses other people's good intentions to knock us off course and hold us back from fulfilling our destiny. You may relate to this: You're all fired up and got a clear vision of some aspect of your future, and you know what you need to do. You may be excited or at least feel hope arising, and even though what you're about to do is challenging and will take a big step of faith on your part, you're sure it's the right thing to embark on.

One of the first things you'll probably do is tell a close friend or family member what you're planning. And the next thing, this person who wants the best for you is telling you how you need to be careful, that what you're planning is unlikely to work and they begin giving you their advice, which on the surface appears to be wisdom, but leaves you feeling deflated.

Yes, it's often good to share plans with a friend and take godly counsel, but beware – the enemy seems to enjoy speaking through other people's 'wisdom', and he'll do it in such a way as to deceive you into thinking it has come from God. Fear can masquerade as 'wisdom'.

The enemy wants to chip away at our faith and lead us to believe that perhaps we were mistaken and before we know it, we're beginning to believe his lies and give up.

Jesus had this happen to Him. He shared with His best friends what He was about to do, and on the face of it, Peter gives 'godly' wisdom but even goes so far as to rebuke Jesus…

"From that time on Jesus began to explain to his disciples that he must go to Jerusalem and suffer many things at the hands of the elders, the chief priests and the teachers of the law, and that he must be killed and on the third day be raised to life. Peter took him aside and began to rebuke him. "Never, Lord!" he said. "This shall never happen to you!" Jesus turned and said to Peter, "Get behind me, Satan! You are a stumbling block to me; you do not have in mind the concerns of God, but merely human concerns" (Matthew 16:21-23).

On the face of it, Peter appears to be saying the right thing; not wanting Jesus to be killed. But this was contrary to Father God's plan for Jesus, and Peter was in fact speaking out the devil's plan for His life. We see that as soon as Jesus discerned that it wasn't just Peter speaking, but an evil spirit speaking through him, immediately Jesus rebuked the devil and did not come into agreement with what had been spoken.

We too can learn from Jesus in this way. Peter was not in tune with God's heart here, but was responding out of human thinking which Jesus recognized as even being demonic. It seemed like wisdom for Peter to declare that something 'bad' was not to happen to Jesus, but actually it was a spirit of fear speaking through Peter.

It is so important to know God's heart and to be obedient to Him, through faith, and to discern evil spirits when they are at work, even through those closest to us.

IN EVERYDAY SITUATIONS

From 'gremlins' in our car or washing machine, to accident-prone family members, business failures through to chronic health problems and premature deaths, demons have a lot to answer for!

We shouldn't attribute every difficult circumstance to a demon directly, of course. Since the 'fall' in the Garden of Eden, all humankind including all of creation has lived under 'the curse'. So it's not surprising that bad stuff happens around us from time to time. However, the good news is that God loved the world so much that He sent His only begotten Son Jesus Christ to earth as a man, to die in our place and to save us from our sin and bring us into right relationship with God. I'll share more on what that means in another chapter and how we can be free, but for the moment let's look at other ways in which demons can affect our lives.

DEMONS CAN AFFECT OUR HEALTH

Demons can afflict us in many ways. Matthew 12:22 tells of a demonized man who was blind and mute and when he was set free from the demons, he could see and talk! Often physical symptoms have a spiritual cause. In Matthew 17 we read of a boy who had seizures caused by a demon. As soon as Jesus rebuked the demon and cast it out of the boy, he was healed of the seizures.

I was speaking at an event we hosted recently and during the opening session a boy was causing distractions. His height and stocky build belied his age of ten, so I thought he was much older. His mother sat directly in front of me but the boy would not sit still. He was climbing on the table, then he came up next to me on the stage, all the while shrieking in a high pitched squeal and gnawing on a leather belt. Despite being

112

just a boy, he seemed to have extraordinary strength and could not be moved easily. We discovered later that he had been diagnosed with severe autism. He was unable to speak and had not uttered a word since birth, just this strange noise.

It was very distracting and the next morning as I was speaking about the power of the cross and the blood of Jesus, he continued to shriek and disturb not just me, but the attendees too. I felt badly, but while preaching I had to ask his mother to take him out into the lobby. As soon as I had finished my session, I went into the lobby to talk to her. I gave her a hug and prayed for her – I can't imagine how hard it must have been to parent him. The boy was charging around the place with no one able to calm him down.

With help from others, I managed to get near and pulled the leather belt from him. Apparently he would always gnaw on any belt he could get his hands on, and I felt it was something he needed to be free from. I knew it was a demon causing the problem, so very gently but firmly I told the demon to leave him at the name of Jesus and not to touch anyone else. We released the presence of Jesus into his life through the Holy Spirit and invited the Prince of Peace into his mind, his emotions and his body. He sat down and a sense of peace seemed to come over him.

I had to go back into the conference, but apparently

the boy was calm and stopped running around and the constant shrieking had ceased. He sat quietly for the remainder of the event and also while we baptized his mother along with many others. The following evening as I invited people to come and share what God had done over the weekend, this same boy came up to the front with his mother. He was calm, he no longer held a belt, he gave me a hug, and in tears, his mother told us that he had spoken for the first time in his life. He said 'mama' along with other words. Weeks later she wrote and told us he is developing well and is now the best behaved of all her children. She was healed of a physical condition at the event and her marriage was restored. When she got home, she was leading other people to Jesus, praying for work colleagues and witnessing miracles of healing. This is the truth: no matter what or how severe the condition or situation, the power of Jesus brings wholeness and freedom.

Luke 13:16 tells the story of the woman 'bound by Satan' for eighteen years who had a 'spirit of infirmity' or 'spirit of disability' that caused her to be bent over. Crippling spirits of disability are still causing havoc today and no amount of surgery or medical intervention will bring full healing if the illness has a spiritual cause. What is needed is to be rid of the evil spirits causing the problems and for instant healing to come through the power of Jesus, just like He did for the woman in Luke 13.

If you have any kind of disability, then please don't feel ashamed or offended or think I'm saying that you are demonized. You are no less loved by God or less able in the kingdom of heaven. Not all disabilities are caused by evil spirits. But what I am sharing is spiritual truth which has the power to set you free and whether your condition is caused by an evil spirit or not, you can still be healed through the power of Jesus Christ.

THE POWERFUL PRESENCE OF GOD

I have noticed that sometimes when I'm near a person who is demonized, they begin to get agitated, start sweating, run away, feel dizzy or sick. One time I was chatting to a woman in our Blacon café. The previous Sunday she had visited our meeting but told me that the presence of God was so strong she had raced out of the building and down the road, despite using a walker because of her deformed feet!

But in the café she told me she wanted to follow Jesus. We invited her to pray out and invite Jesus into her life, but she clutched her head and said she felt confused. I explained it was a spirit of confusion and that she could tell it to leave in the name of Jesus, which she did, and then she was able to ask Jesus into her life. We also prayed for her deformed feet and next time we saw her she showed us how she was completely healed. They were no longer deformed; the pain was gone and she had no use for her walker or stick. (She also brought her daughter into the café who was instantly healed of a long-term back injury. This happened the moment the daughter said she would drop a court case where she was suing her employer for compensation for the injury).

PHYSICAL MANIFESTATIONS OF EVIL SPIRITS

Over the years, we have witnessed some crazy manifestations by demons and no doubt, as you continue to follow the Spirit of Jesus, you will too. Perhaps you've had some of these things happen around you and wondered what they were. As a follower of Jesus, there is no need to fear, but to calmly help the other person to get free. If you have any strange manifestations begin to happen in your body or weird feelings caused by demons, then simply tell those demons to leave you and for Jesus to come and fill you with His Spirit.

Some of the reactions we've come across are as follows:

When mentioning the blood of Jesus or even saying His name, a person nearby beginning to shake or curse. Going near to a demonized person with a Bible and the person's body contorting to get out of the way of it. We gave a young lady a Bible once and it vibrated so violently in her hands she had to throw it back to us! We've had expressions of hatred when confronted with the gospel of Jesus, seen people's faces contorting, shape shifting, eyes bulging, strange voices speaking through the person, shrieking and screaming, paralysis of limbs, cramps, convulsions, symptoms of epilepsy – writhing on the floor, foaming at the mouth, slithering like a snake, barking like a dog, eyes rolling back in their sockets, head shrinking, person suddenly looking very old, being thrown to the ground, attempting to strangle themselves or harm themselves, violence towards others, falling on all fours on the floor, claiming to be the beast or a demon named in the Bible, speaking lies about those around them, supernatural strength that even the police cannot deal with, incessant talking, talking about their sexual exploits or fantasies, appearing unconscious, sudden acute symptoms such as appearing to have an asthma attack, stroke, loss of consciousness, seizure. Wild eyes, sudden pain, something looking or feeling like it's poking through the skin, hives or some other apparent allergic reaction, heart palpitations, dizziness, sudden confusion, foul smell and so on. Other manifestations of demons can include lying, cursing, blasphemy, criticism, accusation, fault-finding, gossip and mockery.

Being full of the presence of Jesus can cause demons in people around you to manifest. The person near you may look confused or get hot and start sweating, they may have an intense pain in the head, rub their arm, run away, begin to argue, shout, look like they are going to vomit, fall asleep or any other unusual reaction.

As soon as you see something like this, if possible, ask them what the problem is or what they're feeling. They will usually be open with you and tell you they have a sudden headache or they need to leave quickly or they have a strange sensation in their legs or may feel faint. I would then ask if it feels good or bad. If it's good I explain it's probably the Holy Spirit, the presence of Jesus they are feeling. If it's bad, I tell them that the presence of Jesus is making any evil spirits uncomfortable and if they want to be free of those demons, now is a good time to get rid of them!

Of course, if the person is shouting, getting violent or unable to speak for some reason, don't delay but immediately speak to the demon and tell it to stop what it is doing and either to leave or to let the person speak. Be led by the Holy Spirit and do and say what you feel He is showing you. If in doubt, ask for help.

Sometimes when a demon manifests, it isn't so obvious. One day a woman came into our Blacon café with a friend. While they were waiting for their food, she told us she'd broken her ribs. We prayed, she felt her ribs move back into place, the pain left and she said she was healed. Her friend had broken her arm, so we prayed for that and the same thing happened. The friend said she wanted to know Jesus, but as their food had just arrived, we said we'd pray with her after they'd eaten.

The first woman was asking a lot of questions about Jesus, and in answer to one of her questions, I said that as followers of Jesus, we have the power to raise people from the dead. At that, she stood up, her demeanor changed and she began to get angry. She was shouting at me in front of other customers, she grabbed her friend and stormed out, telling passers-by that they mustn't go into our café. I felt humiliated, upset and shaken. Afterwards I realized it was just a demon manifesting. What I should have done was to take authority over it, speak to it and either tell it to come out or be quiet in the name of Jesus.

Mostly, I was upset that the woman's friend had not had the opportunity to give her life to Jesus. Amazingly, a few months later, the Lord reminded me of her, so I prayed that she would meet someone who would lead her to Jesus. An hour or so after I prayed, I went to our local supermarket and was surprised to see her standing by the checkout. She told the friend she was with how Jesus had healed her broken arm, and as we stood in the supermarket car park holding hands, they both gave their lives to Jesus and the friend got free from a spirit of kleptomania!

Of course, we don't go looking for demonic behavior. It's helpful to know how to recognize it and what to do when it manifests, but we keep our eyes focused on God's kingdom realm. Here, **"The fruit of the Spirit is love, joy, peace, forbearance, kindness, goodness,**

**faithfulness, gentleness and self-control"
(Galatians 5:22).**

SEEING IN THE SPIRIT REALM

Many years ago, I was sitting on the sofa chatting to my husband Rob, when out of the corner of my eye I saw a huge black shadow moving across the room and it went behind the sofa. I ignored it, but after a few minutes I told Rob that I was feeling unwell. All my joints began to ache and I felt very tired. I decided to go and lie on the bed upstairs. As I was lying there feeling ill, a strong thought, like an inner voice came into my head, "Satan take me!" The evil spirit had settled on me and wanted me to speak these words out loud; it was quite forceful. I was incredulous and could not believe the impertinence of the thing! I found it difficult to speak but I said, "How dare you. Leave in the name of Jesus now." Instantly I felt well again. I wasn't sure how a demon thought it could get away with being so brazen about it, but I realized I was learning something about the enemy's ways of working.

DISCERNMENT OF SPIRITS

The following story may also help you understand how demons operate. One day as I was working in our Blacon café, I got chatting to a customer who told me that she'd suffered from a stroke about six months earlier. So I asked if she'd let me pray for her and she agreed. As I was telling the stroke symptoms to leave her body through the power of Jesus, I heard my name being called from the other side of the cafe. "Aliss, Aliss! Help me!" I looked across and saw a Christian man I knew who had just walked in. I ran over as he was shouting, "I'm having a stroke."

I concluded it must be demonic and that perhaps it was an evil spirit that had caused the woman to have a stroke six months previously and now that same spirit had left her and was having a go at this man. I quickly encouraged him to tell that spirit to leave and as soon as he did this, all the symptoms left, just as suddenly as they had appeared. What interested me was that he could easily have succumbed to the symptoms and had a stroke. I wonder how many people are living under something like depression or sickness when if they recognized it for what it was, they could be free through the power of Jesus? The more we come into agreement with the symptoms, feelings and pain caused by a demon, the more that evil spirit has a hold on our lives. And often it will invite more demons to join it.

POLTERGEISTS AND GHOSTS

Penny from Wales, one of our first Coaches to run Spirit Lifestyle Classes, shared this story with me: "A friend of mine owns a manor house which she and her husband run as a guest house. She had been experiencing odd things happening there, and parts of the old building made her feel uneasy. She asked me to join her in praying around the building and grounds.

The current manor house was built in the late 18th Century on the site of a medieval manor which was frequented by men of the Knights Templar over a long period of time.

We walked around the house and listened to the Holy Spirit as we prayed and declared in each room until we felt the atmosphere change. We went into a particular room and shared about Jesus and commanded the spirit to go to Him. My friend affirmed the bedroom felt fine after that.

On the large landing we shared the gospel of Jesus and sent all the spirits to Him. At one end of the manor was a small room on each floor. These were the sluice rooms and each one felt spiritually dark and oppressive although they were not physically dark rooms. We cleansed these from all evil spirits. A cellar door off the kitchen seemed to have a pull on us. I had the sense of a servant having been thrown in there as a punishment and forgotten about. I don't know if that was true, but we prayed accordingly anyway.

Soon after that some 'Angel Worshippers' came and were mortified at the change in the atmosphere of the place, and what had we done with all the 'angels' who used to sit along the ridge of the roof?! They offered to come back as a group and try to get them back again. No thank you! The 'Angel Worshippers' didn't come back.

We returned a while later to pray in the woods and grounds concerning the Knights Templar aspect. We brought salt and wine as we felt led to by the Holy Spirit (Jesus says we as His children are salt on the earth and wine represents His blood). As we walked, we constantly asked Holy Spirit to guide us and reveal to us what we needed to do. We prayed, sprinkled salt and the blood of the Lamb for cleansing...

There have been no more 'occurrences' at the manor. All seems good."

Very often, ghosts and poltergeists are simply evil spirits that may have been attached to a person or sometimes to a place where a traumatic incident or demonic activity has happened in the past. The best thing to do is for you as a follower of Jesus to reveal the light and power of Jesus wherever you go and any evil spirit, any darkness will leave. It may manifest first, as we've already discussed, but you simply tell it to leave and not come back.

THE POWERFUL LIGHT OF JESUS

Now let me share with you a wonderful story about

Viv and what happened to her some years ago. Following Jesus brings the light into every place you go, including your home.

Early one Sunday, soon after we had started a new church in Blacon, Chester, I was preparing for speaking that morning. I asked the Holy Spirit to give me words of knowledge for people who would be there in the service. I was alone in my bedroom but I heard something moving in the wardrobe next to my bed. It sounded as though someone was moving all my shoes around. Then a similar noise occurred at the foot of the bed. I wasn't scared, but I was rather curious.

Later that morning after I had preached, I said, "Is there anyone here who has strange things happening in their house, like a poltergeist?" A woman sitting on the back row whom I did not recognize, raised her hand and said, "Yes, it's me." She came out to the front and told us that there was a poltergeist in her home that had been there for the past three years. She was so scared she'd decided to go to church that day to see if God could do anything. She had also arranged for a psychic medium to call round at her house that afternoon to try and cleanse it.

I explained that if she gave her life to Jesus, the demonic activity in her house would stop, so she did. She prayed out loud and invited Jesus into her life as everyone watched and cheered. She then went home, prayed round her house and telephoned the psychic medium. She cancelled her appointment and told him that his services weren't necessary as she had now found Jesus and said, "What you're doing is wrong; you need Jesus too." Needless to say, she experienced no demonic activity in her house after that.

I later realized it must have been an angel in my bedroom that gave me a word of knowledge that day by making all that noise!

If you have any strange occurrences in your home like Viv had, I recommend doing what she did: ask Jesus into your life and as you reveal the light of Jesus, you will find any evil spirit has to leave. The gospel of Jesus is about true spiritual freedom and joy in the Holy Ghost.

CHAPTER SEVEN

Closing Demonic
Access Points

Having encountered many people over the years wanting to be set free, it seems that demons often enter a person's life during their childhood or adolescence. Demons take advantage of times of weakness and this can be anytime from conception onwards. Even during conception, if the father or mother of a child is demonized, then that child can also be affected by the same demons. If a woman is raped, a demon of violence and others can pass from the rapist to the woman and to her unborn child.

Any woman who has an unwanted pregnancy can invite a demon of rejection to enter her baby, particularly if she wants to terminate the pregnancy or has negative feelings towards the child in her womb. A child is dependent upon its parents for protection, and if that protection is not there for whatever reason, then a door is left wide open for evil spirits to invade that child.

Mandi, who you may have read about in my book 'Unexpected Miracles' attributed her life of heroin addiction, violent crime and prostitution to what happened to her before birth:

"My mother met my father when she was twelve. She was crying at a bus stop and he pulled over in his wagon and befriended her. He preyed on the vulnerable and groomed my mother from the age of twelve. By fifteen she was pregnant. She went on to have four children by the time she was nineteen, but my father was married with six other children... I think my problems began even before I was born. For some reason, I repeatedly kicked my twin sister when we were together in our mother's womb. She was born black and blue, and as a result, needed to be kept in hospital for three weeks after delivery. I didn't do it on purpose, but my mum took an instant dislike to me and didn't pay me much attention because of it; I felt such guilt."

Miraculously, after decades of a life of crime and drugs, Mandi met Jesus one day in our Blacon café and her life changed dramatically. All the guilt, the shame, the addictions and darkness left her when the light of Jesus came into her life.

HOW DEMONS GAIN ACCESS

Demons look for a door that is open into our lives, no matter how small. We may have done something to invite a demon in or perhaps it has seized the first opportunity it can to enter. They don't need to be invited twice! Demons choose the weakest moments in our life to gain access and aim for our weak points as they attempt to take control, often paving the way for other demons to enter too.

A huge problem we face in our society today is of children feeling abandoned or not wanted. With more than half of marriages ending in divorce and the general breakdown of family life, feelings of rejection in children is very common. Evil spirits of rejection use these opportunities to gain entry to a child's life, and can be followed by other spirits such as self-loathing, hatred, bitterness, anger and sometimes suicide. This perhaps explains why the suicide rate in young people is so high, in fact according to the American Psychological Association (www.apa.org), suicide is around the tenth leading cause of death across all ages in the United States.

The act of abortion can invite a spirit of death into the life of the mother, the ones performing the abortion and even the father if he is in agreement with the abortion. History shows that the shedding of innocent blood through the sacrifice of children during rituals was a source of demonic power for those practicing it. Today, through abortion, those demons are still active.

I heard of one young woman who became pregnant by accident. Both she and her partner made the decision to abort the baby. But as she approached the abortion clinic, even just to enquire, she heard screams in the spirit realm and felt the presence of the spirit of death so strongly that she ran away from that place as fast as she could. She went on to have the baby and now, happily married, their children are a source of great joy.

But for those who have had abortions, many face guilt, shame and regret, and can be plagued by thoughts of suicide, ill health, fear and depression.

I recently met a lovely woman who told me that she had been struggling with guilt and shame for over 50 years since having an abortion as a teenager in the 1970s. The only person who knew about the abortion was her husband and I chatted to them both soon after they'd been to our workshop. The lady was happy to let me video (you can watch it on my YouTube channel) as she shared her testimony for the first time, in the hope that someone hearing her account could be helped:

"I was prayed for at the workshop and Jesus set me free from the shame and the guilt that I have carried for over 50 years. It had kept me from becoming a Christian for all those years as I didn't see that God could accept me after what I'd done. I lived in fear, guilt and shame for all this time.

Until now, I struggled with knowing I was forgiven and couldn't forgive myself either. But through the Spirit Lifestyle workshop and the lady who had a word of knowledge for me and prayed with me, I have been set free. It is such an amazing feeling to know that God accepts me and He loves me. He has forgiven me. And my child is waiting for me in God's kingdom." How wonderful that there is freedom, healing, forgiveness and acceptance through the blood of Jesus.

FAMILIAR SPIRITS

Demons will often try to jump from one family member or close friend to another. The first funeral that my husband Rob conducted was sadly for a twenty-one-year-old who had taken his own life. At the wake after the funeral, we talked to a friend of the family whose wife had also committed suicide that same week. Then we spoke to a young man who told us that at the same time his friend had died, he had attempted to kill himself, but was unaware of his friend's death until later. This seemed to be more than simply a 'coincidence'. Harboring feelings of rejection, abandonment and despair can open a door to spirits of suicide.

There is a small town in South Wales which had a phenomenon where teenagers were committing suicide at an exceptionally high rate. From 2007-2008 it was reported that 26 young people, mainly teenagers, had committed suicide in the small town and during each of the ten years prior to this, an average of 3 men per year had also taken their own lives. The police could find no link between any of the deaths (stats from Wikipedia, People magazine and 2013 TV documentary 'Bridgend'). To this day no-one knows why all this was happening, but it was likely to be demons of suicide wreaking havoc in that place and something or someone would have invited them in.

The good news is that since this time, the Spirit of Life (see Romans 8:2) is setting people free from the spirit of death in that place as many churches are springing up in the area and even missionaries have been sent there, demonstrating the love and power of Jesus and releasing His Light in what used to be a dark place.

As followers of Jesus, we are given spiritual keys to the kingdom of heaven that we can use to lock out death and bring life. Jesus said: **"…And on this rock (of the revelation of Jesus Christ the Son of God) I will build my church (my people walking in authority), and the gates of Hades (death) will not have power over it. I will give you the keys of the kingdom of heaven; whatever you bind (prohibit) on earth will be bound in heaven, and whatever**

**you release on earth will be released in heaven"
(Matthew 16:18-20).**

As we submit to the authority of Jesus and live in union with Him, we can use the keys of the kingdom of heaven wherever we go, to lock out death, disease and destruction and to release life in all its fullness. This is the new model; this is what we are called to walk in and there are people whom God is raising up all over the earth that are beginning to live like this. I pray that you will be one of them.

If you identify a familiar spirit in your family; premature deaths, addiction, anger, fear, gossip, pride or whatever may have attached itself to your family line, then you can cut it off through the blood of Jesus. If necessary, confess the sin of your family and stand in the gap, asking God for His mercy, forgiveness and freedom. I have included prayers in a following chapter that will help you to do this.

ANGER

The sin of anger (as opposed to righteous anger in line with God's heart) can open a door to a spirit of anger which may manifest in fits of rage. Evil spirits seem to work in groups, and often one evil spirit operating in someone's life can open a door to many more. For example, a spirit of anger if left festering can make way for spirits of revenge, hatred and even murder to enter a person's life. Often a murderer will say that 'something came over me and made me do it' or will complain of hearing voices telling them what to do and they will sometimes have no recollection of the act itself.

The Bible says not to sin in our anger. What keeps us from sinning when we feel angry is to identify with those with whom we are angry. It is okay to get angry with some injustice or with what the enemy is trying to do, but be careful not to get into accusation and criticism of others.

Drunkenness can open a door to evil spirits. Living God's way is wisdom: **"Don't get drunk with wine, which is rebellion, instead be filled continually with the fullness of the Holy Spirit" (Ephesians 5:18 TPT).**

A VICTIM MENTALITY

Some psychologists such as Freud teach that we are a product of others' behavior and thus shift the blame and responsibility for our own bad choices or responses onto others. "I have mental health issues because so and so did such and such to me" or "I have anger or addictions because so and so left me or told me such and such which made me feel rejected".

But the problem with this way of thinking is that if we shift responsibility for our actions, emotions or unhealthy lifestyle onto another person or situation, then it becomes our identity. It is very difficult to instigate any change if we believe the problem is not ours. Jesus said that the thief, Satan, comes to 'steal, kill and destroy' and often he does this through our responses to circumstances and challenges we face. If we come into agreement with Satan through bitterness, resentment, fear, hatred and so on, we inadvertently open access points in our lives for evil spirits to enter.

It is important that no matter what has been done or said to us in the past, that we break away from the demonic power and do not give it a place in our lives. Choosing not to be a victim, we surrender our thoughts, emotions and will to Jesus so that we can be empowered by Him.

The real truth is that the choices we make in how we react and respond to difficulties in our lives set the course for the rest of our existence. No matter what was said or done to us in the past, it's done. It's time for us to let that go and if you follow the principles and the activations in this book, then you can be free from the past and right away begin to live the life you were created for. No more delay. No more regrets. No more anger, bitterness or hatred. No more fear, rejection, inner pain or turmoil. It's your choice.

LEARNED BEHAVIOR

Many people unwittingly think that a way they behave is simply a personality trait when it is in fact a learned behavior and quite possibly a demon. Criticism, anxiety and so on can be dealt with, so don't always assume that certain emotions or ways of thinking are simply down to 'just the way I am'.

Other sinful behavior such as lying, stealing or cheating, can open the door to a lying spirit, a thieving spirit, a cheating spirit and so on. This can make us vulnerable, even for a split second, to evil spirits gaining entry.

PHYSICAL AND EMOTIONAL TRAUMA

Accidents and any other trauma, such as abuse, can unfortunately allow evil spirits into our lives, even through no fault of our own. If we have surrendered our lives to Jesus Christ, obedient to His Word and full of His Spirit, then we come under His protection. But as soon as we let our guard down, we can allow spirits of fear, trauma, infirmity or others to gain access into our life.

I was speaking at a large conference in South Carolina and at the end of one of the sessions as I stepped down from the stage to pray for people, I came face to face with a severely demonized woman. I recognized right away that the problem was spiritual and as the demons began screaming and trying to intimidate me, I calmly took authority and commanded them to leave. One of the demons was a spirit of trauma.

The powerful story is described by the woman herself as she later shared on the video we took of the incident (you can watch it on my YouTube channel). It demonstrates not only what demons are capable of, but more importantly, the tremendous power and authority of Jesus:

"I had sensory processing disorder for years after a traumatic incident as a child. My father tried to kill me and my whole family before the age of two. I was unable to let anyone touch me ever since I was a little child and I made life hell for those around me. I was visited by demons, I had nightmares for decades. I couldn't stand music or wear certain materials. Sounds would trigger an attack so I couldn't go out to a restaurant or buy groceries. The slightest thing would startle me.

The condition kept me isolated and controlled my life. I didn't know it was caused by demons until now! I realize it was demons that wanted to control not just me but everyone around me. Aliss has helped me. The demons have left me and I feel like a weight has been lifted. I feel lighter, I feel better, I feel more in my own body. I feel good, I feel grounded. I'm free." AJ

SEXUAL IMMORALITY

Sexual promiscuousness, adultery, pornography and so on, can open a door to demons such as lust, lies, perversion, soul ties, addiction and shame. Sadly, instead of the personal freedom that such behavior seems to advocate, those involved can find themselves bound in lifelong regret and guilt; leaving a trail of failed marriages, unwanted pregnancies and broken hearts, they are anything but free. Some sexual demons even cause the person's voice to change pitch and for certain mannerisms to manifest in that person.

In casual relationships, men sometimes use the promise of love to get sex and women often use sex to try and gain love, even without realizing it. Both can lead to heartache, poor consequences and not to mention, demonization.

Often in the Bible demons are called 'unclean spirits'. This can refer to sexual demons as well as others. There are accounts in the Old Testament of fallen angels procreating with humans. If any type of spirit that is contrary to the Holy Spirit enters your bedroom, simply tell it to go, no matter how loving it appears or how lonely you may feel. Many have shared with me how they are subject to unwanted demonic visitations at night and are desperate for it to stop, despite allowing it at first. Thankfully, through the power of Jesus, the demonic entrapment can be broken.

SOUL TIES

'Soul ties' refers to where an unhealthy attachment is formed between two or more people. It can happen if a gift is exchanged that binds a person to another, a vow made to an individual or a group, a past commitment to a partner or lover, or a pact that is made for some reason. Any demons that are active in that person's life potentially can have access to us if we have not confessed any sin and broken any ties we have with them spiritually.

This can also happen if a husband and wife separate and I have come across it between a parent and child, for example a mother not allowing her adult son to be fully independent. If that person or group still has some control over our lives, or we cannot seem to get over the break up of a relationship - there is no closure no matter what we do, or the feelings are still raw years later, then it could be that a soul tie needs to be broken. This can be done through confession to God and repentance, severing ties through prayer, and any gift, jewelry or object connected with them destroyed or returned.

ADDICTION

A spirit of addiction can enter by taking addictive substances such as smoking, using drugs, excessive alcohol and of course gambling. However, a spirit of addiction can also enter through 'harmless' activities such as eating food, social media, TV, shopping, sex, work or any other activity we do, if we do it in order to fulfill a need in our life in the wrong way.

You may find it helpful to think of the times you feel 'stressed' or 'depressed' and what you find yourself doing. Write down if you 'need a drink' or 'need to go shopping' or 'need some comfort food' or whatever it may be for you. Ask the Holy Spirit to show you what triggers that feeling and that He would expose it for what it is.

Perhaps you have a deep-seated sense of 'rejection' or 'lack of self worth' or some other soul issue. That is the root of the problem, so allow the Lord to deal with that and once it is unearthed, freedom can come quickly.

Let's look at an example of how a spirit of addiction can gain entry into someone's life: A person enjoys a relaxing treat - it's pleasurable - whether eating chocolate, purchasing new clothes, having a beer, or enjoying some erotic sequence in the latest TV streaming series.

When experiencing a stressful time the person thinks, 'What I need is a treat - I deserve a treat - I need to relax' and so they have another beer or chocolate, watch more of that sensual TV, or spend more money on clothing.

Now the evil spirit of addiction sees a potential weakness there, so it thinks "Aha... that's your thing; let's focus on that!"

So, for a while, the person continues getting their treat when they feel like they deserve it, and the demon is patient, just making small suggestions: One more drink, one more purchase, why not surf the net for more erotic entertainment? Only, the treat is gradually getting more intense, more 'needful' and more demanding.

Instead of a piece of chocolate, now they regularly need a whole bar, now the unworn clothes build up in the wardrobe or instead of one or two beers with friends they begin to drink wine and spirits at home alone.

Now the evil spirit really has some hooks in them. Now it suggests that what they really need is much more than is decently 'allowed' or permissible... it suggests that it's best for the person to gratify their 'needs' in private.

Then they have a full blown secret addiction; superficially they are fine and seem happy, but in private they are an enslaved addict and completely miserable, living in spiritual and mental conflict. The evil spirit has made itself at home and no matter what they try, they cannot get free.

If that describes you, or someone you know, then do keep reading, because identifying the problem is half the battle. As the Spirit of God is enlightening you through this book, then the steps in the following chapters will help you gain complete freedom. Of course, once you are set free from a spirit of addiction, you will still need to make the right choices, and we shall also cover that later in this book.

PHYSICAL CONDITIONS

Many physical conditions and illnesses can be caused by demons and we have already covered some of these in a previous chapter. Coming into agreement with an illness or diagnosis in any way can compound the matter and can give the evil spirit a 'legal' right to take up residence. I have known of people who have been so worried they may get a certain disease that a door is opened into their life to a demon of fear and then other demons of the very disease they feared. I would advise against continually speaking negatively about a condition or telling others all our problems, as that seems to empower evil spirits.

Over years of praying with others, I have noticed that anxiety, stress and fear can open a door to a spirit of fear which can cause some allergies and conditions such as asthma, food intolerance, digestive disorders, phobias and so on.

We were hosting a Spirit Lifestyle workshop in West Virginia and one of the participants had a serious allergy to peanuts. She told me later how she loved Reese's Peanut Butter Cups but had not been able to eat any for years – the allergy was life-threatening. As I was sharing this insight about food intolerances and allergies, the woman's throat began to scratch, just as though there were nuts nearby and she immediately realized it was a demon manifesting in her body because the truth had been exposed. During the practical activation, she asked God to forgive her for coming into agreement with that evil spirit and she told it to leave at the name of Jesus. She felt it go and decided to test out her healing. On the way home that evening, she stopped at a grocery store, bought some Reese's Peanut Butter Cups and consumed the whole pack! She returned the next morning to tell us that she had no symptoms and was free of that debilitating condition. The cause was simply a demon. (NB. We had not told her to do that; if she had asked, we would have suggested she seek medical advice first – and we recommend you do the same - but it was definitely a step of faith).

GOSSIP AND ACCUSATION

Many years ago, a woman came to visit me. She had been a Christian for twenty or thirty years and was an active member of a previous church we had attended. Sitting in my living room with coffee in hand, she spent most of the time gossiping about church members. I didn't like the way she was talking and so as soon as I could, I got up and made my way to the front door, indicating it was time for her to leave.

As she was talking in the hallway, I watched wide eyed as her head began to shrink smaller and smaller, her features contorted and deep wrinkles appeared on her face and neck. So much so, that she looked to be about 150 years old!

I saw all this happen with my eyes; it wasn't a vision but was actually happening in the physical realm. I felt an evil presence. I'd never seen anything like this before and didn't know what to do. If it happened now, I would probably just tell it to come out in the name of Jesus, but I was so shocked, all I could say was, "Well it was nice to see you, goodbye" and I was thinking, "Don't call us, we'll call you!" Just then, Rob came back from work, walked past us both, said "Hi" and went into the other room.

Eventually I managed to usher her down the steps and into her car before closing the front door and praying around the hallway as I could still feel the evil in the house. Shocked, I walked into the sitting room and remarked to Rob, "You should have seen what just happened!" to which he replied, "You mean the way her head shrank and she looked really old? I knew you could handle it, so I left you to it!" Thanks Rob!

Demons are ugly, and in this case wrinkly, and if we don't want to look like one, perhaps we should stop the accusations and the gossip!

COMPLAINING, CRITICISM AND PRIDE

The Apostle Paul tells how the Israelites of the Old Testament grumbled and complained as they wandered through the wilderness. They ignored the faithfulness and goodness of God and because of their grumbling, took themselves out from under the protection of God and they were killed by a destroying angel (1 Corinthians 10:10). It is wisdom therefore, to stay in step with God, and to be careful of what comes out of our mouths.

Negative speaking, criticism of others and pride are all thoughts and actions that can attract demons. At a workshop we hosted in California, a supernatural word of knowledge was given by an attendee during a practical activation. The word was for someone who was very 'critical' towards others and a man humbly came out in response. I have transcribed his words from the video we took at the time:

"I have been hurt a lot and gone through a lot of rejection in my life and I had become very angry about it all and was very critical. I was beaten by my father until the age of five, then my stepfather abused me emotionally for about forty years and I had problems seeing myself in a good light. I became critical of God and other people as I was not able to receive break-through. I also had chronic migraines for 25 years." We gave opportunity for others in the workshop to stand if they too had been critical of others, and then asked if the man was willing to pray.

He continued: "Father I ask you to forgive me for my criticism that has come through rejection and for all the hurt. Forgive me for every evil word spoken out of my mouth and for my anger and also for coming into agreement with the enemy and all the poison spoken by me and the hatred."

I led him and others in the room in a prayer: "Thank you Father for forgiving me. I renounce every evil spirit of criticism, hatred, rejection, anger etc and I rebuke it and command it leaves me now in Jesus' name." I suggested that people take a deep breath in of the Holy Spirit and then said "1-2-3 out. Evil spirits leave. We break off every assignment of the enemy against your life by the blood of Jesus. Migraine headaches and any evil spirits causing those must leave now in Jesus' name. Tormenting spirits go." People began to cough and get free. I told everyone to put their hand on their heart and released the Father's love through the Holy Spirit to do a deep work.

The guy began to cough as demons left and then uttered a loud, deep cry as the pain and the trauma of the past left along with the evil spirits. Afterwards he shared how the Holy Spirit had told him that morning that he was going to be healed of the headaches and set free that day. We were all humbled by the wonderful kindness and love of God displayed that afternoon.

Jesus says, **"To him who has, more will be given" (Matthew 13:12)** and **"Where your treasure is, there your heart will be also" (Matthew 6:21).** Whatever we treasure is what we attract. So, if in our hearts we grumble and complain, not only will we attract other people who grumble and complain, but we will also attract more problems for us to grumble and complain about. If we value gossip, we attract gossip. Like attracts like. If we have anger towards a political party for example, we will attract other people and circumstances that reinforce our resentment. The measure we give, will be measured back to us.

POVERTY

There is a spirit of poverty and it can attach itself to us and our families if we worry about money or if we withhold what belongs to the Lord. It can also gain access if we do not have a giving heart; are miserly or greedy. If you seem to always be struggling with finances and no matter what you do or how hard you work, you never seem to have enough, then a spirit of poverty may be present. Of course, we also need wisdom in the way we spend money; we want to be good stewards of what God entrusts us with.

In addition to repenting and getting set free, choosing to be generous and giving to others will keep the spirit of poverty away. Saying, "I can't afford this or that" or "I can't do what God's asking me to do because I don't have the money" can attract the spirit of poverty. Instead, by following the Holy Spirit and living by faith, we can choose what to spend money on and what not to. And if God is leading you to do something that you feel you cannot afford, take that step of faith and trust Him to come through. John Wimber, founder of the Vineyard Movement said: 'We give to get to give.' In that way you will overcome a spirit of poverty and you will find that the money is there when you need it.

FEAR AND ANXIETY

Did you know, the most frequent command in the Bible is do not fear, do not be afraid? It must be for a reason. God knew we were going to face many challenging situations. Jesus said **"Do not be afraid..."** **(Luke 12:32).** The original Greek word in this verse for 'afraid' is the word 'phobeo' which is where our word phobia comes from. Jesus continued, **"...The Father has been pleased to give you the kingdom"**. Fear is one of the main ways the devil stops us moving forward into God's plan for our lives, but the truth is, it's the enemy who is afraid of us as we extend God's kingdom here on earth. He is afraid of us knowing our true identity as children of God and walking in that authority and power.

I have heard Bill Johnson of Bethel Church, Redding, say, "You can recognize what the enemy fears in your life by what he attacks. And when he fears you discovering something, he often attacks it." The nation of Israel in the Old Testament did not inherit their promises and walk in their inheritance because they feared what lay ahead and they did not trust God.

Let's consider a present day example of how a spirit of fear or anxiety can enter a person's life: A woman has a big shock when her husband suddenly dies. She grieves but she's okay. Then one day while in the shopping mall she has a health scare - she feels dizzy, her heart rate suddenly goes up and she feels unwell. Panicked, she gets checked out by the doctor. He tells her she's fine and that she must have had a panic attack which is understandable since she's just lost her husband. But he prescribes her some tablets to calm her nerves.

The next time she needs to go shopping she is driving to the mall and begins to feel fearful: 'What if it happens again?' This voice is coming from a spirit of fear and inadvertently she agrees with the spirit: 'Yes, best not go there – it would be better to go to the smaller local shop.' However, as she parks her car, the spirit puts thoughts in her head: 'Is that your pulse going up? This is too risky, it would be best to go home.' If she comes into agreement with that spirit, within a few months she may find that she has full blown agoraphobia and cannot even leave the house at all.

Evil spirits usually begin subtly, but as we come into agreement with them in any way, not only do we empower them in our lives, but we open a door for other evil spirits to join them. Before we know it, we find ourselves imprisoned, controlled and mani-pulated by demonic forces, without even realizing it.

When I'm reading Scripture, I often like to find out the meanings of the words in the original written Hebrew or Greek. Recently I looked up Philippians 4:6,7 and using the original meaning of the Greek it reads: 'Do not be anxious about anything... but let the peace of God which transcends and completely surpasses all understanding - your intellect, your mind and all of your thoughts, feelings and desires - protect (like a military garrison and guard to prevent hostile invasion) your heart (physical and soul), your mind, your thoughts and your purpose in Christ Jesus.' As I meditated on this, I felt myself lifted up and encompassed in His peace, transcending all of the chaos going on around me at the time. We can learn to live in this supernatural peace but it doesn't happen automatically, however it's something we can practice and enjoy each and every day as we submerge ourselves in Jesus.

"God will never give you the spirit of fear, but the Holy Spirit who gives you mighty power, love and self-control (the Aramaic can also be translated 'revelation-light'). So never be ashamed of the testimony of our Lord... but overcome every evil by the revelation of the power of God" (2 Timothy 1:7,8 TPT).

CHAPTER EIGHT

The Power To Break Free

A demon can only have power in our lives if we come into agreement with it in any way. As a child we should come under our parent's protection – sadly not all parents act wisely, plus there are unforeseen circumstances that also can happen. Then as an adult, we make our own choices. If a parent died young or there is a hereditary disease or addiction in a family, then very often, the grown-up child will begin to fear the same thing happening to them. Demons play on this and will put thoughts into our minds. When we come into agreement with the enemy and his plan for our life, we are empowering the evil spirits and providing an open door for them to enter. Before long, we may begin to experience the same symptoms or behavioral traits we dreaded.

It is important not to come into agreement with fear but to embrace our Heavenly Father's love for us and to trust Him with our lives: **"There is no fear in love.**

But perfect love drives out fear" (1 John 4:18).

Fear and anxiety can cause many illnesses and can kill. I've known people who have worried so much about getting cancer or some other disease that they have ended up getting the very thing they dreaded.

THE POWER OF AGREEMENT

In ancient times there was a man named Job (pronounced Jobe) who was wealthy and blessed in every way and seemed to have everything going for him, but then things changed and he had terrible calamities befall him. He lost everything; his family members died and he himself was very sick.

Job remarked, **"What I feared has come upon me, what I dreaded has happened to me" (Job 3:25).** From this statement, we see that Job feared the worst. Fear is the access point for the thief to enter. The enemy (and his evil spirits) can only have power in your life if you allow him or come into agreement with him and his evil plans. Job must have come into agreement with the enemy's plan for his life; to steal, kill and destroy him and his family. The Bible says that Satan approached God and asked permission to attack Job. I believe the reason God allowed it was because Job was in agreement with Satan, albeit unwittingly. However, God would not permit Job to be killed. Perhaps Job was not in agreement with the devil's plans for that to happen, but that which he did fear, Satan was permitted to carry out.

If we can receive this revelation about the power of agreement it could change our lives. If we come into agreement with Satan's plan for our lives, God has ordained that what we fear will be fulfilled. The Bible says, **"The highest heavens belong to the Lord but the earth He has given to mankind" (Psalm 115:16).** God has given us authority over what happens on the earth (see Genesis 1:28).

GOD HAS A GOOD PLAN FOR YOUR LIFE

If we come into agreement with God's good plan by the way we think and act, we will see that fulfilled in our lives as we keep following Jesus and submitting to Him and His ways. Jesus said, **"Truly I tell you, whatever you bind on earth will be bound in heaven, and whatever you loose on earth will be loosed in heaven. Again, truly I tell you that if two of you on earth agree about anything they ask for, it will be done for them by my Father in heaven. For where two or three gather in my name, there am I with them" (Matthew 18:18-20).**

This is powerful truth and we need to understand this revelation. Think about it. The enemy often works like this: An evil spirit comes to you but is very subtle. You come across news articles or social media posts about the likelihood of you developing a serious disease or you have a genetic history of something in your family, or you google symptoms that you are experiencing in your body.

Your mind latches onto those 'facts' or possibilities and the evil spirit whispers to you that perhaps you have that disease or could do so in the future. You don't realize it's an evil spirit as it seems to be your own rational thoughts, seemingly real symptoms or even words from a person you respect. You read stories or hear doctor's advice to go for certain tests or to check yourself out regularly. Each time you do this, you think something may be found, and you begin to worry. You start to imagine the scenario in your head and start to plan what you would do. While all this is happening, you are coming into agreement with that spirit of fear, that lying demon which is manifesting in your mind or your body.

WHY DO BAD THINGS KEEP HAPPENING?

We just read the Scripture that if two agree on earth about something, it will be done. We can bind something and stop it from happening and we can agree with it and cause it to happen. This can occur for good or for evil. Jesus said that He would be there when we come into agreement with Him, but the converse could also be true. Evil spirits are attracted when we come into agreement with the enemy. Not only can we empower evil spirits in our lives, but they often attract their cronies too, and we may find that one thing after another is coming against us, and a never-ending battle ensues.

So just as with Job, if we come into agreement with a demon that 'such and such' may happen to us or we may have 'such and such' in our mind or our body, that demon then has permission to make it happen. Because God has put earthly things under our authority (Genesis 1:28), even God will not prevent that thing from happening if we've come into agreement with it. In His wisdom, God has made us extremely powerful in this way. I may be begging God to free me or heal me of something, but if I'm the one that has opened a door to the evil spirit that caused the problem in the first place, then I'm the one who needs to deal with it.

IT'S MY CHOICE

As with most things, I have a choice. I can choose to disagree with those demonic thoughts or actions and 'bind' them from having any power. I can choose to believe that God's word is true, that what Jesus did and said was not just for two thousand years ago, but He is the Living Word and is still powerful. His immense power is available to us today.

So let us make that decision; that we will choose to

break agreement with the enemy and with his evil plans for our lives, and choose instead to believe God and come into agreement with His good plan and purposes as we seek to follow Him.

THE ULTIMATE SOURCE OF POWER

In order for us to be set free from demons and break the power and curse of Satan over our lives, we need to know the ultimate source of power; the true and Living God. Once we understand His love and His power, and all that Jesus accomplished for us when He came to earth, we are then able to apply that to our lives. As we do this, it will change us forever and bring freedom, wholeness and life in all its fullness.

Understanding what Jesus accomplished on the cross and through His resurrection is key to getting free and living a powerful, overcoming life. The best way to receive this wonderful revelation is to read the life-transforming Word of God (the Bible) and to encounter Jesus personally. In this chapter I have included many Scriptures and I encourage you not just to read them, but to let the truth of the words permeate your spirit, your soul and your body.

These truths alone contain the power to set us free and as we invite the One in whom these words originate into our life, His very presence breathes and fills us with His liberty. **"Where the Spirit of the Lord is,**

there is freedom" (2 Corinthians 3:17).

So, I make no apology for the number of Scriptures I've quoted here, for in them and in the Living Word Himself, is the answer you've been looking for! The Word of God is the Truth and contains the power by which we can be free and live free. It may be helpful to read aloud the Bible verses that I've quoted. I have altered the tense of some of the verses slightly to make it more personal to you as you read them.

Declarations spoken out loud are powerful in the spirit realm and as you do this it will also help to get the truth deep down in your soul. If any demons try to prevent you from reading this in any way, simply call on the name of Jesus and keep going until you can read them all.

I pray that you will believe the truth contained in these verses and apply it to your life. But don't make the mistake of simply knowing about the truth, this is an invitation from heaven for you to KNOW the Truth. He is a person. When you KNOW Jesus, He will set you free and as you continue in Him, you will stay free.

Jesus came to earth as a sinless man, and in sub-mission to Father God, He took on ALL our sin, our guilt, our rebellion, our sickness, our pain and even the curse of death itself. ALL evil and, get this - even our old evil self - was nailed to the cross with Jesus as He surrendered His life for us (see Galatians 2:20). He paid the price for our sin and all the effects of sin, and when He died and through His subsequent resurrection from the dead, the power of Satan including the power of sin, sickness and death, was broken once and for all.

Powerful declarations for you to recite:

THE POWER OF THE CROSS

"Jesus Christ shared in my humanity so that by His death He broke and utterly destroyed the power of him who holds the power of death—that is, the devil— and freed me from a life of captivity and fear of death" (Hebrews 2:14).

"If I declare with my mouth, 'Jesus is Lord,' and believe in my heart that God raised Him from the dead, I will be saved (from sin and death, delivered from demons, healed, made whole and kept safe)" (Romans 10:9).

"The message of the cross... is the power of God" (see 1 Corinthians 1:18).

On the cross, a divinely ordained exchange took place. All the evil due to us came upon Jesus, so all the good available to the sinless Jesus was made available to us who believe. That is the grace of God.

THE POWER OF THE RESURRECTION

"Jesus Christ, who being in very nature God, did not consider equality with God something to be used to His own advantage; rather, He made Himself nothing by taking the very nature of a servant, being made in human likeness. And being found in appearance as a man, He humbled Himself by becoming obedient to death - even death on a cross! Therefore God exalted Him to the highest place and gave Him the name that is above every name, that at the name of Jesus every knee should bow, in heaven and on earth and under the earth, and every tongue acknowledge that Jesus Christ is Lord, to the glory of God the Father" (Philippians 2:6-11).

"Having disarmed the powers and authorities (of evil), He (Jesus) made a public spectacle of them, triumphing over them by the cross" (Colossians 2:15).

Father God "...raised Christ from the dead and seated Him at His right hand in the heavenly realms, far above all rule and authority, power and dominion, and every name that is invoked, not only in the present age but also in the one to come. And God placed all things under His feet and appointed Him to be head over everything..."
(Ephesians 1:20-22).

RESCUED AND FORGIVEN

"...I give joyful thanks to my Father God, who has qualified me to share in the inheritance of His holy people in the kingdom of light. For He has rescued me from the dominion of darkness and brought me into the kingdom of the Son He loves, in whom I have redemption (been set free), and the forgiveness of sins" (Colossians 1:12-14).

Jesus surrendered His life so that we can live a life of freedom and fullness in union with Him and inherit all that He is and all that He has.

CHOOSE LIFE

In Deuteronomy 30:19 we read how God gave the people a choice: **"Today I have given you the choice between life and death, between blessings and curses. Now I call on heaven and earth to witness the choice you make. Oh, that you would choose life, so that you and your descendants might live!"**

Just like the Israelites in the Old Testament had a choice, we still have that choice to make each and every day of our lives. If you choose life, then as you read this, speak out loud the words: **"I CHOOSE LIFE!"**

As you do this, you may feel something beginning to

happen. Repeat those words until you mean it and you may notice a shift take place in the atmosphere around you.

JESUS IS THE ANSWER

Mirjam, one of our Spirit Lifestyle Coaches, shares how she got free from demons:

"Soon after I gave my life to Jesus, I attended a Spirit-filled church. A person was sharing a story about casting out a demon from someone's house. Right after that, something grabbed my throat and pressed hard. I found myself running to the front of the church.

The force inside of me threw me on the floor and I started convulsing. Four people came around me and commanded the evil spirit to go. Someone asked, "Is she a believer?" I was new in that Church so they didn't know me. Someone who had met me said yes. They started to rebuke the spirit in me even more. And then it was like an invisible 'hammer' from Heaven hit me on the head! I felt the power of God going in from my head pushing down the evil thing. I never screamed but I yelled, "Get out of me, get out of me!" And then I saw a dark shadowy witchlike figure leave me; an awful creature.

After that I felt so heavy. Like every muscle in me had

relaxed. My body felt like dead. (Just like the Biblical account in Mark 9). Someone said, "Pick her up." And they sat me on a chair and prayed some more, but I knew it was done! I felt so light and sooo happy! I used to have visitations from witches when I was a young girl; they would inflict pains of all sorts. I did not know how that door was opened, but I dealt with it all my life, till that glorious day of deliverance! Jesus set me free! That was almost 20 years ago. Jesus frees people from demons. Oh, the wonderful power of the Holy Spirit!"

And that same power is also available for you today. In fact, **"…If the Spirit of Him who raised Jesus from the dead is living in me, He who raised Christ from the dead will also give life to my mortal body because of His Spirit who lives in me" (Romans 8:11).**

JESUS IS THE HIGHEST POWER

Through Jesus we have the power to break free simply and quickly, once and for all. And we no longer need to be subject to demonization in the future. You can apply this next verse to your own life as you read it:

"The reason the Son of God (Jesus) appeared was to destroy and completely undo the devil's work (in my life)" (1 John 3:8).

"And Jesus went through all Galilee preaching in their Synagogues and casting out the demons" (Mark 1:39).

"The 72 returned with joy and said, Lord, even the demons submit to us in your name" (Luke 10:17).

"All authority has been given to Jesus in heaven and on earth" (Matthew 28:18).

THE NAME OF JESUS IS POWERFUL

Keep reading these verses aloud if you can. Remember, I have changed the tense where possible so you can receive the powerful truth for yourself.

"And these signs will accompany me as I believe: In His name I will drive out demons... I will place my hands on sick people, and they will get well" (Mark 16:17).

Jesus has "given me authority to trample on snakes and scorpions (evil spirits and sickness) and to overcome all the power of the enemy, nothing will harm me (if I remain in Him). I do not rejoice that the spirits submit to me but rather I rejoice that my name is written in heaven" (Luke 10:19).

"You are my King and my God who decrees victories for me. Through you I push back my enemies, through your name I trample the foe" (Psalm 44:4,5).

"Thanks be to God! He gives me the victory through our Lord Jesus Christ" (1 Corinthians 15:57).

"At the name of Jesus every knee shall bow, in heaven and on earth and under the earth..." (Philippians 2:10).

SUPREME POWER IS IN THE BLOOD OF JESUS

Communion is extremely powerful when we understand the significance behind it. Jesus told us to eat the bread and drink the wine in remembrance of Him. As we do this, we are recognizing what He accomplished on the cross when His body was broken and His blood poured out for us.

The act of communion is not simply symbolic, but speaks to the spirit realm of the ultimate power and authority of Jesus. When we participate in this by faith, there are heavenly implications. If you have chosen to follow Jesus, then I encourage you to take communion as often as you like. It doesn't have to be limited to church meetings, but we can take communion with a friend or family member as we pray together, or with a meal, just like Jesus did with His disciples.

Following are a few of the many Scriptures that

help explain the power that is contained within communion. Again, I have slightly changed the verses so they are personal as you read them aloud:

"I overcome the accuser (Satan) by the blood of the Lamb (Jesus) and the word of my testimony and by surrendering my life to Jesus" (see Revelation 12:11).

"If I walk in the light, as He is in the light, I have fellowship with others, and the blood of Jesus purifies me from all sin" (1 John 1:7).

Jesus said, "This is my blood of the covenant" - which was poured out for me for the forgiveness of my sins" (Matthew 26:28).

"Since I have now been justified (just as if I never sinned) by His blood, how much more shall I be saved from God's wrath through Him!" (Romans 5:9).

"In Him I have redemption (Jesus has paid the price and bought me) through His blood, the forgiveness of sins, in accordance with the riches of God's grace" (Ephesians 1:7).

"Jesus made (me) holy through His own blood" (Hebrews 13:12).

"How much more, then, will the blood of Christ, who through the eternal Spirit offered Himself unblemished to God, cleanse my conscience from acts that lead to death, so that I may serve the living God!" (Hebrews 9:14).

"Since I have confidence to enter the Most Holy Place by the blood of Jesus, by a new and living way opened for me through the curtain, that is, His body, and since I have a great priest over the house of God, I will draw near to God with a sincere heart and with the full assurance that faith brings, having my heart sprinkled to cleanse me from a guilty conscience and having my body washed with pure water" (Hebrews 10:19-21).

CHAPTER NINE

Breaking Curses And Strongholds

The Bible talks about 'powers and principalities' over regions (see Ephesians 6) and in the book of Daniel we read how the Archangel had been held up answering Daniel's prayer by the 'Prince of Persia' - a spiritual principality over a geographical region.

In a recent live Q&A webinar on our training portal, we were asked how to pray against such demonic spirits over geographic territories and how to remove them effectively. I would counsel against randomly battling with them directly and to only do what the Holy Spirit clearly shows you. Prayer is essential and the Bible exhorts us to pray, but the way we pray is very important, and we must always be led by the Holy Spirit in this.

Jesus told us to **"cast out demons"** and to **"trample on**

snakes and scorpions" which represent evil spirits (see Luke 10). He delegates His power and authority to us to do that as we submit to Him. Demons are territorial, and they want the territory and the inheritance that has been given to us by God. Demons will go after that territory and once they have it, are reluctant to let it go.

However, in the gospels, we don't see Jesus commanding principalities over regions to leave. In the story of the demonized man of the Gadarenes, when the demons came face to face with Jesus, they knew they were about to be driven out of the man. However, they asked not to be sent out of the region, but to be allowed to inhabit a herd of pigs nearby. Even Jesus did not command them to leave their territory, but simply to leave the man so that he was free and at peace (see Mark 5). Incidentally, often demons don't seem to like water (and in Matthew 12 Jesus said they try to find dry places) so I think it's quite ironic that not only did Jesus send the demons into non-kosher pigs but they all ran into the sea and drowned!

In Mark 6, we read that Jesus was unable to perform miracles in his hometown because of the spirit of unbelief permeating the place. But did Jesus confront the spirit of that area by commanding it to leave? No, He simply continued with His mandate from heaven.

Even when Jesus was faced with the temptations of

the devil himself in the wilderness, He did not put God to the test but only spoke God's words of truth. He submitted completely to Father God and continued with His assignment. It would be wise for us to do likewise. As we surrender our lives to Jesus, just as He surrendered all to Father God, then we too will overcome the enemy, and come out of the wilderness time of testing, like Jesus, **"in the power of the Holy Spirit" (Luke 4:14).**

OUR MANDATE FROM HEAVEN

Jesus commissioned his twelve disciples and sent them out with this mandate: **"As you go, proclaim this message: 'The kingdom of heaven has come near.' Heal the sick, raise the dead, cleanse those who have leprosy, drive out demons. Freely you have received; freely give" (Matthew 10:7,8).** He gave a very similar mandate to His seventy followers (see Luke 10) and Jesus still commissions us with the same mandate today (see John 14:11,12).

Reading Luke chapter 10, I can just imagine the seventy followers of Jesus feeling a sense of trepidation as they went off to proclaim the good news of the kingdom of heaven, healing the sick and casting out demons. I'm sure they were wondering what would happen and how they would get on. Amazingly they came back from their adventure **"full of joy and said, 'Lord, even the demons submit to us in your name.' Jesus replied,**

'I saw Satan fall like lightning from heaven. I have given you authority to trample on snakes and scorpions and to overcome all the power of the enemy; nothing will harm you. However, do not rejoice that the spirits submit to you, but rejoice that your names are written in heaven'" (Luke 10:17-20).

It is worthy of note that as the disciples were driving out demons from people and healing the sick, Jesus declared that He saw Satan fall like lightning. He did not instruct His followers to seek out and pray against Satan or any principality, but He sent them out to extend the kingdom of heaven, and as they were doing this in submission to Jesus and through His power, the enemy fell.

In Jeremiah 1 we read how the prophet was commissioned by God to **"uproot, tear down, destroy and overthrow."** But at the same time, his mandate was to **"build and to plant."** If the enemy's stronghold in a region or in a person is uprooted and overthrown, we must ensure that the building and planting of God's kingdom becomes established there.

THE SAFEST PLACE TO BE

Soon after we'd started a work in Blacon, a 'deprived' neighborhood of 18,000 people in our hometown of Chester, UK, the 'Prince of Blacon' appeared to me one night; I assume it was trying to intimidate me. My first thought was we must have rattled it for it to appear like that. Demons tend to manifest when they feel threatened, so I took that as a good sign that we were doing what we were supposed to be, and in the right area. As the prophetic author Rick Joyner often says, "The safest place to be is at the center of God's will."

WARRIORS RUN TO THE SOUND OF BATTLE

I was contacted by Satanists in the area who were checking us out and was told that we were on their 'patch' but I didn't succumb to the intimidation.

Demons are after your territory; your purpose and destiny and the sphere of influence you're called to - family, work, ministry and so on. I believe that is one of the reasons the Prince of Blacon manifested as it did.

However, at no time did the Holy Spirit tell us to pray directly against that territorial spirit. In fact, the Holy Spirit had been leading me to pray for Satanists, witches and Spiritualists in the area, that they would know the love and power of Jesus and follow Him. We were privileged to lead a number of them to Jesus over the twelve years we lived in Blacon.

As well as praying for people involved in the occult to know Jesus and be set free, the Lord also encouraged us to keep doing what we were doing: sharing the good news of Jesus wherever we went, healing the sick, casting out demons, resurrecting people from the dead (I've been down the mortuary a few times!) and generally demonstrating God's love and power to those we met (see Matthew 10). We were also going all out with worship and prayer too.

Hundreds were giving their lives to Jesus as a result and we were baptizing and discipling them. We opened a miracle café in the heart of Blacon, as well as a community church, a weekly School of the Spirit and we helped whoever we could.

As a result, the crime rate went down, house prices soared, new ministries were birthed and I knew we'd gained spiritual breakthrough in a place that formerly had no hope. Even the name of the place meant 'dark pool' but we knew that by bringing the light of Jesus, the darkness and the spiritual principalities had to flee.

We recently met up with the young man who was the first to be healed in our Blacon café. He was the troubled teenager the police warned us about; he'd dropped out of school and was causing mayhem in the neighborhood. When we first met him, he'd fallen off a roof and broken his ankle, but as we prayed, the bones moved back into place and the pain left. Not long after this healing, he and his friends asked Jesus into their lives and at the same time, the spirit causing ADD left him too.

It was so good to see him again after all these years and we had a great time reminiscing. Incredibly, he shared all the things that have dramatically changed in his life since he chose to follow Jesus. He is full of peace, he went on to attend college and is now the owner of a very successful roofing company – quite ironic since it was a roof he'd fallen off when we first met! This is just one of the many lives transformed in Blacon, as we continued to focus on all that Jesus had called us to do.

JESUS TEACHES ON DEMONS

The teaching of Jesus on demons in Matthew 12 is an interesting one, and even though He's speaking of a person, I believe it can also be applied to a region:

"When an impure spirit comes out of a person, it goes through arid places seeking rest and does not find it. Then it says, 'I will return to the house I left.' When it arrives, it finds the house unoccupied, swept clean and put in order. Then it goes and takes with it seven other spirits more wicked than itself, and they go in and live there. And the final condition of that person is worse than the first."

My feeling is that if we were able to command a territorial spirit over a region to leave, then if that area were not full of the presence of God and submitted to His authority, that principality may go, find its cronies and come back to that area, resulting in a worse condition than before.

The region would need to be full of people extending the kingdom of heaven in all areas of society and taking their rightful authority there spiritually. But if we begin to do what Jesus commissioned us; that is, proclaim the kingdom of heaven and, following the way of love, cast out demons, heal the sick, raise the dead and so on, the territorial spirit will be displaced and the area occupied by God's kingdom. This is a far safer and more fruitful way of doing things. So do whatever the Lord shows you and you won't go far wrong.

WHAT IS A STRONGHOLD?

A stronghold is like a fortress or a castle. Something that is built and fortified to keep territory protected from outsiders. We have many castles here in Wales, and in the spirit realm there are demonic strongholds as well as godly ones. So a demonic stronghold is where the enemy has taken territory in a geographical region or sphere of influence, or in an area of our life. This could be in our spirit, soul or body and he does this so he can gain ground and destroy us and our relationships, including our relationship with God. He will lie to us and cause us to lose, or not be aware of, our true identity as a powerful child of God. When we believe the lies of the enemy, he adds another brick to his stronghold. Believing the lie empowers the liar.

I've quoted this Scripture already, but here it is again, this time from the NIV translation: **"For though we live in the world, we do not wage war as the world does. The weapons we fight with are not the weapons of the world. On the contrary, they have divine power to demolish strongholds. We demolish arguments and every pretension that sets itself up against the knowledge of God, and we take captive every thought to make it obedient to Christ"**
(2 Corinthians 10:3-5).

By putting in place the revelation of truth shared in this book, you can expect strongholds of the enemy that have been built in your life to be demolished by divine power. Then you will know the truth and the truth will set you free. The weapons of our spiritual warfare are divine power, that is, the power of God, and we read in 1 Corinthians 1:18 where the source of that power comes from:

"The message of the cross is foolishness to those who are perishing but to us who are being saved it is the power of God."

The message of the cross is powerful. It is the power of God and in the next few chapters we will look more closely at what that means for us and how we can apply that to our lives and receive all that Jesus has made available to us through His death and resurrection.

RECOGNIZING CURSES

Some years ago, I heard on the news that a young mother on a UK reality TV show had spoken something racist about one of the other contestants. Men became incensed in the nation about which she had made the comment and I watched with concern as they burned placards and effigies of this young woman. In effect they were cursing her.

At the time, I told my husband Rob, that this young mother was in danger of receiving those curses and I hoped that she knew Jesus personally and was able to protect herself by faith through Jesus' blood. However, as far as I knew, she did not have a personal relationship with Jesus.

I wanted to help as I could see what was happening in the spirit realm but had no access or any way to contact her; she was a 'celebrity'. Soon afterwards she was diagnosed with cancer and died in just a matter of weeks, leaving a husband and two young children. Such a tragedy and something that could have been prevented.

I cried out to God that He would allow me to become a voice; that what He had shown me over the years about spiritual realities could be learned by others. I hope that by writing this book it will help you understand the truth about the spirit realm, that you would encounter the Highest Power of the universe (who is a person: Jesus) and learn how to apply what you learn to your own life and share with those around you.

THE EFFECTS OF A CURSE

We can be living under a curse but not know it. Perhaps you are?

Some of the ways curses can come are:

Through our family lines (generational curses), from witchcraft, spells, occultic blood curses and the like, through soul ties, through people speaking negatively about us or self-imposed curses where we speak negatively about ourselves, sustained belief of the enemy's lies or actively disobeying God.

In the Bible, there are certain indicators that could suggest someone is living under a curse. Identifying one or two from this list does not necessarily constitute a curse is present, but if many of these have occurred in one person or one family for no apparent reason, then it is likely a curse needs to be broken.

I have taken the list below from the following Scriptures –
Deuteronomy 28, Genesis 3, Galatians 5. Make a note of any from this list that you can identify with:

- Repeated or chronic sickness or hereditary illnesses
- Repeated miscarriages, inability to conceive, reproductive problems
- Mental or emotional breakdown
- Breakdown of marriage and family relationships
- Continual lack of finances and/or unemployment
- Accident prone
- Addictions
- History of suicides or premature deaths in the family
- Confusion, inability to think clearly or see a way out
- Long term depression

Several of these in one person or family indicates a curse is likely to be at work. If you can relate to the following verse from Deuteronomy 28:

"**...Unsuccessful in everything you do; day after day oppressed and robbed, with no one to rescue you**" then you too could be living under a curse.

But we have a choice - we can choose life or death, blessings or curses. **"This day I call the heavens and the earth as witnesses against you that I have set before you life and death, blessings and curses. Now choose life, so that you and your children may live and that you may love the Lord your God, listen to His voice, and hold fast to Him. For the Lord is your life" (Deuteronomy 30:19,20).**

Perhaps you were told repeatedly as a child that you weren't good enough or not clever like your brother or sister. Or that you would always be fat or unattractive or always be a failure. Words are powerful and can have a devastating effect, particularly when you are growing up and needing acceptance and love. If you choose to believe the negative comments spoken over you, then that can open a door to evil spirits entering. You may have been wondering why you seem to fail at everything you do, or that you can't lose weight no matter how hard you try. Once you get free from those spirits, things should get easier.

We can curse people by the words we use. "You stupid girl", "You'll never have any money" or other such phrases that easily come out of our mouths, can profoundly affect those people for the rest of their lives. It is also easy to curse oneself with phrases such as, "I'm worried to death", or "I'm sick and tired", "I'll always be fat" or "I'm a failure". Make the decision now that you are not going to do this any longer and expect to see a difference in your life and your relationships.

The Bible tells us clearly that **"the tongue has the power of life and death" (Proverbs 18:21).** The words we speak can literally bless or curse others and even ourselves. We must watch what we say.

One way we can nullify a curse is by following the

teaching of Jesus. **"Bless those who curse you, pray for those who mistreat you" (Luke 6:28).** This does not mean that we come into agreement with the negative voices. Nevertheless, we do not retaliate or look for revenge, but if a curse is heading your way through the words or actions of another, then we can break its power by submitting to the Lord and releasing God's blessing for that person. You'll see how to do that when we come to pray in a moment.

THE GOOD NEWS!

When Jesus died on the cross and rose again, he broke the power of the curse: **"Christ redeemed us from the curse of the law by becoming a curse for us, for it is written: "Cursed is everyone who is hung on a tree" (Galatians 3:13).**

You may have heard me tell the amazing story of Terry 'Fingers' who came into our Blacon café one day. He was a local character and the first time I met him he told me a gypsy had cursed him some years before. Now if you're a follower of Jesus and someone curses you, you can simply brush it off and not let it land on you. I may say something like, "By the blood of Jesus (or through the name of Jesus) I don't receive that" and don't give it any more thought.

But whether you follow Jesus or not, the more you give that 'curse' room in your life by thinking about it, talking about it or believing it, then it has power over you and will affect you – it's as though you give it a legal right to be there.

Anyhow, back to Terry. I told him I could pray for him, so he let me pray and I told any curse to leave him through the blood of Jesus. He then explained how glass had been deeply embedded in each of his fingertips for a number of years. I told all the glass to leave his body and not to cause any pain as it left. The following day he came back into the café and showed me how not only had all the glass left his fingertips supernaturally, but a tiny piece of glass had exited his foot too. He hadn't known it was there but it had caused him pain for 30 years!

GENERATIONAL CURSES

Rob and I had been invited to speak in Aberystwyth, Wales, some years ago. It was a few hours' drive and we only just got there in time! We made our way to the front of the meeting and began to speak. A woman came up and told us how she had problems with her legs and feet and couldn't walk far. She thought she'd been cursed some time previously and asked us to break it off her. As we did so, her twelve-year-old daughter at the back of the room started shrieking and ran down to where we were standing.

She told everyone how infected eczema had caused

her skin to be broken, bleeding and itchy. Incredibly, at the same time we broke the curse off her mother, the girl felt the power of God go through her body and the bleeding, scaly skin immediately transformed before her eyes and became smooth and new like that of a young child. She was showing everyone in that place what had happened, and as mother and daughter hugged, the mother also realized she was healed of her leg and foot problems too.

If a curse is causing you sickness, once you release yourself from the curse, healing quickly follows.

In the Old Testament, we read how actively disobeying God can bring a generational curse onto a family for three or four generations. However, in the next sentence, God declares that He demonstrates His love **"to a thousand generations of those who love me and keep my commandments" (Exodus 20:5-6).**

You may have come from generations of occult, freemasonry, addiction, violence, abandonment, failure, religion or whatever, but when you turn to God and follow Jesus, any and every curse can be broken and in turn, your whole family line becomes blessed.

FAMILIAR SPIRITS

A familiar spirit operates when someone in a family

opens a door to demons in their life. This can then affect other family members, even down through the generations.

It could be that someone in your family has been involved in some kind of sin, whether that be Freemasonry, the occult, addiction or whatever. That sin can open the door for demons to come in and attach themselves not only to that family member, but to the family line. Or a curse may have been declared over your family by someone who has spoken negatively of you, or like the celebrity I mentioned earlier, by someone who wants you harmed.

As a follower of Jesus, you don't need to worry about curses coming at you, but if the Holy Spirit shows you, then just bat it away and don't give it a place to land, or a foothold. The less focus you give it the better.

"Like a fluttering sparrow or a darting swallow, an undeserved curse does not come to rest and has nowhere to land" (Proverbs 26:2).

It wouldn't surprise me if curses - whether word curses, blood curses or whatever - are carried by evil spirits to their target. So for a curse (or evil spirit) to impact you, it needs to have a place to land where it can gain a foothold. Sin and even fear in your life is like having a huge landing strip with flashing lights directing the demons in to land.

Additionally, coming into agreement with that demonic thing in any way, shape or form, is like opening a wide doorway into your life and inviting it in.

OVERCOMING THE CURSE OF SIN AND DEATH

Since the fall of mankind in the garden of Eden, ageing, decay and death are a 'natural' part of our lives and the world around us. But I want to tell you that this is one of the ways the devil has us living under a thick veil of deception; a 'death shroud' as it were.

Adam and Eve in the garden did not believe the truth of God's word: "Do not touch or eat of this one tree as you will surely die", and instead they came into agreement with Satan when he told them "You will not certainly die". They ate of the fruit and, instead of the eternal life they were created for, they, and the rest of creation, began to age, to decay and then they died.

THE SPIRIT OF LIFE

Since that time, death has been a normal part of life: **"...Sin entered the world through one man (Adam), and death through sin, and in this way death came to all people, because all sinned..." (Romans 5:12).**

But get this amazing truth: **"For if, by the trespass of the one man (Adam), death reigned through that one man, how much more will those who receive God's** abundant provision of grace and of the gift of righteousness reign in life through the one man, Jesus Christ!" (Romans 5:17)… "Just as sin reigned in death, so also grace might reign through righteousness (right standing with God) to bring eternal LIFE through Jesus Christ our Lord" (Romans 5:21).

A few chapters later, the Apostle Paul writes about God rescuing his body from death. He then continues, **"There is therefore now no longer any condemnation (to death) for those who are in Christ Jesus. For the law of the Spirit of life has set us free in Christ Jesus from the law of sin and death" (Romans 7:24 - Romans 8:2).**

So you see, we are no longer subject to sin and death because as we receive Jesus and live 'in' Him, the Spirit of life - the Holy Spirit, liberates us. But the devil wants to keep us blinded to this fact. So we all go on thinking that we are likely to get ill or have pain as we age, and we just assume that death is inevitable. However, that is not how God created us to be, but if we continue to believe the devil's lies and our minds remain blinded to the truth, then we will continue to be under the power of death.

There are so many Scriptures in the Bible about Jesus breaking the power of death I could go on and on…

"Since the children have flesh and blood, He too

shared in their humanity so that by His death He might break the power of him who holds the power of death – that is the devil – and free those who all their lives were held in slavery by their fear of death" (Hebrews 2:14).

"He has saved us and gave us RESURRECTION LIFE and drew us to Himself by His holy calling on our lives. And it wasn't because of any good we have done, but by His divine pleasure and marvellous grace that confirmed our union with the anointed Jesus, even before time began! This truth is NOW BEING UNVEILED by the revelation of the anointed Jesus, our life-giver, who has ABOLISHED AND DESTROYED DEATH, obliterating ALL its effects on our lives, and has manifested HIS IMMORTAL LIFE IN US by the gospel" (2 Timothy 1:9-10 TPT, NIV & NKJV).

It is time for us to remove that old death shroud once and for all, as we begin to believe the truth that when Jesus died and rose again, the power of sin and death was completely and utterly destroyed.

HEAVEN'S STRONGHOLDS

Just as the enemy can have strongholds and places of authority in people's lives and regions, how much more should the children of God (that's us!) take authority through Jesus in our own lives and families and in the places we live and work. There is no true authority without responsibility, but as we learn to take responsibility for our own lives, our families and communities, we will see the kingdom of heaven - God's kingdom, being established around the world.

Just as we saw a dramatic change in our community of Blacon, we are now helping people around the world raise up heavenly 'strongholds' in their own communities, through our Spirit Lifestyle Classes as well as through Miracle Cafés and businesses, just like the cafés, shops and B&B we established in Chester.

We'd love to help you bring heaven's kingdom realm to your own community, so do get in touch with us if you would like our help. Perhaps you are part of a small group, a prayer meeting, a church or outreach, or have set up a business or some other initiative. Whatever God puts on your heart to be involved in, this is the time to get these established, submitted to the authority of King Jesus and impacting families, towns, regions and nations with the glory of God and His resurrection power!

CHAPTER TEN

Get Ready For Breakthrough!

In this chapter we will prepare for the practical activation we will do in the next chapter that can help you get rid of demons so you can live in freedom. There is no special formula to getting free – as we have seen, it is through the power of Jesus. These steps are simply an aid to help us focus and command demons to leave. As you read, allow the Holy Spirit to speak to you and prepare your heart for the prayers we will pray in the next chapter.

STEPS TO FREEDOM – THE FIVE R'S

Elisha Brown, one of the wonderful Coaches within our organization Spirit Lifestyle, recently shared with us a helpful mnemonic she uses to remember our teaching on getting free from demons. She calls it the 'Five R's':

1. Recognize
2. Repent
3. Renounce
4. Remove
5. Refill

I have used these five headings to help explain the steps to freedom that I've written about. As I have said, there is no set formula when getting rid of demons, in fact I would encourage you above all to follow the Holy Spirit, just as Jesus demonstrated to us in the gospels. However, the following can be helpful and come from years of studying Scripture and our past experiences with helping people to get free.

1. RECOGNIZE

RECOGNIZE JESUS AS LORD

The Lord Jesus Christ is the one whose power and whose blood sets us free from demons, so it's important to not only recognize that Jesus is the way, but also to choose to follow Him and submit to His leadership in our lives.

"Everyone who calls on the name of the Lord (Jesus) will be saved" (Romans 10:13). The original Greek word for saved in this Scripture means saved from sin, healed in spirit, soul and body, delivered from demons and kept safe.

"If you declare with your mouth, "Jesus is Lord," and believe in your heart that God raised him from the dead, you will be saved. For it is with your heart that you believe and are justified, and it is with your mouth that you profess your faith and are saved" (Romans 10:9-10).

So firstly, we must recognize that Jesus is Lord. It's important to know that it is the authority of Jesus that drives out demons. We can't just get rid of them in our own strength or power, or by positive thinking. It's through what Jesus accomplished on the cross, and so in order to be free and stay free, it's important that we submit our lives to Jesus. Thankfully we don't have to be perfect in order to do this; in fact we are made perfect in Him. But now is a good time to choose to follow Jesus each day of our lives.

RECOGNIZE THE NEED TO BE FREE

And of course, in order to be free from demons, we also need to recognize that there is demonic activity in our lives that we want and need to be freed from.

Let us be honest and humble ourselves before God.

"Submit yourselves, then, to God. Resist the devil, and he will flee from you" (James 4:7).

2. REPENT

This book is all about uncovering the enemy's evil plan for our lives, so that we can be freed from his captivity. Satan wants us to keep our sin hidden, in darkness, but until we bring it all into the light, then we remain under Satan's power of darkness. Demons have power in our lives if we come into agreement with them in any way, and by not confessing our sin we give them a 'legal right' to remain. So let us open up before God and be honest.

In my book, 'Unexpected Miracles,' one of the biographies told is of Mark who had been living a lascivious lifestyle of money, sex and drugs. He had also been living under a curse of Freemasonry. Without any idea of what was about to happen, he chose to humble himself and wrote down all the sin he had been involved with. He showed the list to experienced Christian ministers who prayed with him and as a result he was dramatically set free from demons and his life was transformed through the power of Jesus.

"To the humble you bring heaven's deliverance, but the proud and haughty you disregard"
(Psalm 18:27 TPT).

LIVE FROM A HIGHER PLACE

The Biblical word for turning away from sin is to

'repent'. This means turning in the opposite direction from our previous way of behaving and thinking. It is not just a thought but a decision and an action. It means changing what we were doing and living from a higher place. Put off old negative ways of thinking and begin to think and perceive life from a more godly perspective. Instead of attempting to stop thinking in line with the enemy, recognize that we now have the mind of Christ, so begin to think like He does. In this way, we can be full of light, life and creativity.

FREEDOM FROM GENERATIONAL SIN

If the sins of your ancestors have opened a door to demons in your life, then you can release yourself from those sins so they have no power over you, and ask God for His forgiveness. The Holy Spirit shows us what to confess as we ask Him to reveal anything we may have forgotten or not known about.

However, this does not let us off the hook. We mustn't shift the blame onto other people or demons for our own mistakes or even our wrong responses when others have sinned against us. Let's own up and confess it for what it is.

RECEIVE FORGIVENESS

"This is the life-giving message: ...God is pure light. You will never find even a trace of darkness in

Him. If we claim that we share life with Him, but keep walking in the realm of darkness, we're fooling ourselves and not living the truth. But if we keep living in the pure light that surrounds Him, we share unbroken fellowship with one another, and the blood of Jesus, His Son, continually cleanses us from all sin... If we freely admit our sins when His light uncovers them, He will be faithful to forgive us every time" (1 John 1:5-8).

3. RENOUNCE

The dictionary definition of renounce means to 'separate oneself' to 'give up rights' and 'refuse to continue with or abide by'. If we use these meanings in our context here, then we choose to separate ourselves completely from Satan, we cut off all rights that evil spirits have over us, and we refuse to continue allowing demons to co-habit with us.

As well as renouncing the demons themselves, we are to renounce previous sinful practices and patterns of behavior if we want to live a life of freedom.

RENOUNCE FALSE RELIGIONS, NEW AGE PRACTICES AND THE OCCULT

Sever all ties with any religious, 'New Age' or occult practices and groups. Any symbolic items in our homes such as a Buddha, tarot or angel cards, temple items, related books and items of jewelry or clothing, 'holy' books and writings that are not Christian, magazines, clothing and other paraphernalia. Get rid of it all.

Lisa, who also shared her autobiography in my book 'Unexpected Miracles' was a New Age practitioner. She not only asked God to forgive her sin of practicing and teaching Reiki healing, but she gave up her 'New Age' business and closed it down completely. Her life turned around through the power of Jesus as a result and she continues to follow Jesus and is obedient to His leading. When we choose to renounce the powers of darkness, we are making a clean break from Satan and all his works.

CHOOSE TO FORGIVE

Jesus said, **"…If you hold anything against anyone, forgive them, so that your Father in heaven may forgive you your sins" (Mark 11:25).**

If we do not forgive those who have wronged us, we are unable to receive forgiveness ourselves from God. Jesus also makes it clear that if we do not forgive others, we are likely to be held captive in a 'prison' of our own making, even, according to Jesus, being 'tortured' and 'tormented'. This is often the result of demonic activity, brought about by unforgiveness, bitterness and resentment (see Matthew 18:34).

In order to receive forgiveness from God for our sin and be set free fully from evil spirits, it is clear we must choose to forgive all others, no matter what they have said or done to us.

In my experience, one of the main blockages to getting rid of demons, is withholding forgiveness from those who have wronged us. Forgiving can be a difficult thing to do. However, it does not mean that the person who hurt us is being let off, but by choosing to forgive them, we discover that we are the ones who are set free.

We met Mandy at an event we hosted in London and this extract is taken from a post she wrote on our SpiritLifestyle.com community page soon after the event:

"...I had a very serious accident and was left in a wheelchair with catastrophic injuries that meant I lost my career, income and role as active mum. Our lives changed overnight. It seemed that all my hard work had come to nothing... I was physically helpless, and over the next ten years we remained dependent on carers. We were poor, mostly house-bound and life was hard. 'Where are you God?' I would scream when a year later my son became ill and was hospitalized. That's when we discovered that he had a genetic disorder called EDS that had caused my injury too. 'Why? Why? Why God?'...

Then after twelve years of struggle it all became clear to me. I needed to forgive my father - the man who had terrorized my childhood and abused me. I had carried that anger throughout my life like a heavy backpack and it had weighed me down all my life. How could I ask my Heavenly Father to forgive me when I hung on to so much bitterness, both for my father and mother as I felt she had not protected me? Up to that point it felt an impossible ask but now, amidst my suffering, it didn't seem much to ask anymore.

And when I did forgive him, everything changed. I suddenly saw my father through different eyes, felt compassion for the man who had never experienced the joy of loving his children or of being loved without fear by them. My mother had been a victim too so how could I feel any anger towards her? I had carried that fury and rejection with me for over 40 years so it was no wonder I had never found peace!

Quite by chance (what I would call a God-incidence) I stumbled across Aliss and Rob Cresswell's website and decided to go to their Spirit Lifestyle event in London with my disability dog, as I remained tormented by daily nerve pain. At the event my eyes were finally opened as to the power of God's mighty Word and the extent of His unconditional love. I could not deny what I saw unfolding in front of my very eyes through Aliss and Rob's teaching!

I saw so many healings that weekend. Best of all, the chronic debilitating nerve pain that had tormented me for twelve years was healed. I was finally ready to accept His unconditional love and live full time for Him, no longer weighted down by all that anger and bitterness from my past. I was also used as a channel for healing at the event - a woman I prayed for with deafness received her hearing and another was able to walk unaided for the first time in years. Absolute proof that He uses even the least among us! After that time I returned home a new woman in more ways than one."

It is important that we choose to forgive.

4. REMOVE

It is powerful to speak out loud as we deal with demons. We do not need to shout, but the Bible says when we confess with our mouth that Jesus is Lord, we will be saved, healed, set free and made whole (see Romans 10).

We can 'name and shame' the demons! Speak to each one by name if you know what it is – spirit of fear, torment, trauma or whatever the Holy Spirit shows you - and command each one to leave through the power of Jesus.

After naming a demon, resist it and tell it to leave. You may have found reading through this book that demons have been leaving already. That's fantastic, and they cannot stay once you get the revelation of what Jesus accomplished for you personally when He died and rose again! But if you still have some things lurking, don't worry, we'll go through these steps together in the next chapter so you can be completely free.

First, I want to give you some pointers as to how the demons may leave.

HOW DEMONS LEAVE

Demons usually leave through our mouths, but they can sometimes leave through other ways. One time a woman in our shop in Chester felt a spirit of deafness leave through her ear like a whoosh and immediately she got her full hearing back after being totally deaf in that ear since the day her husband died.

Another time, a lady in our Blacon café experienced pain in her arm briefly as a demon left that way after she told it to leave her. Many times I've known people to experience a headache as a demon leaves through their head. But the temporary discomfort should leave as soon as the demon is gone. You can of course tell the demon to stop causing any pain as it goes.

A woman came into our Miracle Café in Bangor, Wales. She began coughing as soon as she walked in the door and I knew demons were already beginning to leave her. She told us she had severe panic attacks that would last for days, there was an evil presence in her home and she had pains in her legs. As we prayed with her and her husband, they confessed to being involved in the occult and then gave their lives to Jesus. As they told demons to leave them, the woman kept coughing and experienced a strong pain like fire in her chest. But she persevered as the demons left her, the pain went, her legs were healed and her face shone with the love and freedom of Jesus. She told us later that the problems had left and she was free.

Demons often cause coughing as they leave, but sometimes seem to get stuck in the throat as they come up; a cough can help to dislodge them. I often tell people to breathe in the Holy Spirit and to breathe or cough out the evil spirits.

Once you've told the demons to leave, stop talking as they come out. Even speaking in tongues while demons are leaving can sometimes get in the way of them coming out.

You may find that you yawn, sigh, breathe, cough, sneeze, laugh, burp, pee or even fart the demons out! There's a hilarious video on my YouTube channel of a pastor who attended one of our events. He had been grieving his mother, but an evil spirit had come in and it had become more of a depression. I was just telling him how the evil spirit was about to leave when he suddenly got hit by the joy of the Holy Spirit. He could hardly stand and as he laughed and laughed the demons left him. We hadn't even prayed or told them to leave! I think that's a great way to get free.

WHERE TO SEND DEMONS WHEN THEY LEAVE

I sometimes get asked if I send demons to any particular place when they leave a person. Scripture is not specific on where to send them, and the best answer is to be led by the Holy Spirit. If you sense from Him that you should tell them to go to a particular place, like Jesus did when He told the demons they could enter the pigs, then do that.

I don't always tell them where to go. But sometimes I will tell them to leave without touching anyone else; other times I may tell them simply to go to Jesus. I figure He knows where to send them, plus Scripture seems to indicate that He likes to keep them under His feet! Jesus **"waits for His enemies to be made His footstool" (Hebrews 10:13).**

REBUKE THE PUKE

I have seen demons try to make the person throw up as they leave or feel nauseous and sometimes a mucus-like substance may come out. If I am with someone who is about to vomit, I often command the demons to come out without doing that. 'Rebuke the puke' is my motto, particularly if there isn't a bucket to hand!

Years ago, when we ran weekly meetings in a bar, a witch gave her life to Jesus. During our Mother's Day service, she began to scream as demons within her reacted to the presence of Jesus. She began to retch just before the children came back into the service. It was quite a commotion with all the screaming and the retching. Right before she threw up and the demons came out, someone grabbed the offering bucket (which was thankfully empty at the time) and got it positioned just in time as she spewed out the contents of her stomach along with the demons with loud screams.

I was at the front with the microphone while all this was happening, and at exactly the same time, the children came back into the room with flowers and cards for all the women. 'Happy Mother's Day' I exclaimed! Our congregation was used to that type of thing, with never a dull moment in our meetings, but even they looked a bit bemused. However, it was wonderful that this mother of five turned her back on witchcraft, gave her life to Jesus and got rid of those demons as her children presented her with flowers and hugged her.

So, sometimes demons leave with a scream or a moan. This is nothing to worry about and is what happened when Philip was in Samaria and people were being set free and healed (see Acts 8). 'Better out than in' - that's what I say! So just go with the flow and keep going if you can until they're all out.

DON'T BE AFRAID

If you have a pain in your body when telling demons to leave, just tell it to go. If the pain moves when you do this, be insistent and tell it to leave in the name of Jesus until it does. Some seem to be more resistant than others.

After demons have left, you may end up on the floor or slumped in a chair and feel quite tired, so give yourself some space, and if you have quite a few to get rid of, you may wish to take a break and resume later. After they've gone you are likely to feel brighter, happier and a lovely light feeling, along with lots of peace and joy, full of life and energy.

At one of our workshops, I'd just finished teaching on deliverance from demons and it was time for the practical activation. People broke into small groups and were beginning to help each other get free from evil spirits. One lady was reluctant to receive help as she was scared she was going to make a noise. However, she'd been telling us how she'd suffered from terrible nightmares since young, and we knew she needed to get free. We encouraged her to receive prayer from another attendee, and as we did, the demons in the woman shouted out, "We've been here a long time – we're not going to leave!" So we calmly told the demons to be quiet and that they were about to go.

We encouraged the lady to confess that she had given these demons a place in her life through submitting to the fear they caused, and she asked God to forgive her. She then told the evil spirits to leave, she took in a deep breath of the Holy Spirit and out they came with a lot of screaming! We told her not to worry, but to just get rid of them. As soon as they'd left, she was like a different person; radiant and full of peace and joy. Those demons of fear had tormented her all her life, but as soon as she humbled herself, took a step of faith and recognized them for what they were, she was free.

Earlier I shared how Adrian who had been a Psychic Medium for years, was set free from demons after meeting Jesus in our Blacon café. The spirit guides he'd been working with turned into what they really were – hideous demonic spirits – after he told them to leave at the name of Jesus. They left without any noise or fuss as Adrian quietly but sternly told them to go. So if you don't notice much as demons leave you, it's OK. You may feel tingling, a change in temperature, a heavy weight or darkness lifting, or you may simply be aware of the Holy Spirit coming upon you and the manifest presence of Jesus around and within you.

Be led by the Holy Spirit as you go through this process, and if you need some help, don't be afraid to ask a Holy Spirit-filled friend or Pastor. We have found that connecting with like-minded people who want to learn how to walk in peace and freedom together is a very powerful and effective way to move forward. There are many ways to do this but if you are interested in connecting with our Spirit Lifestyle members, classes and coaches, we have details at the back of this book.

IT NEED NOT TAKE LONG!

When we read the accounts of people being set free from demons in Scripture, it isn't a long, drawn-out process. Since Jesus has overcome the enemy, and we are set free by His blood and through His powerful name, deliverance can happen quickly.

One of our Spirit Lifestyle Coaches shares how she helped one of her Class members get free. The Class member had recently become a Christian while watching our training videos:

"While praying together, she was aware of Jesus standing in the corner in bright Light the whole time. She told me of several things that had happened in her childhood, including in the womb, then the many occult things she had been heavily involved in, and I wondered where to start! So I asked God to take charge.

After inviting the Holy Spirit, Jesus set to work on all occult stuff while I watched Him at work, amazed. She felt herself blowing up like an enormous balloon, then the air from it was squashed out through her mouth. Then He started setting her free from each of the things and all their attachments one after the other in quick succession... It was astounding to watch the power and speed of Jesus at work."

5. REFILL

Once the evil spirits have left, it is important to be filled with the Holy Spirit; the Spirit of God. Jesus explained what can happen after demons leave: **"When an impure spirit comes out of a person, it goes through arid places seeking rest and does not find it. Then it says, 'I will return to the house I left.' When it arrives, it finds the house unoccupied, swept clean and put in order. Then it goes and takes with it seven other spirits more wicked than itself, and they go in and live there. And the final condition of that person is worse than the first" (Matthew 12:43-45).**

The only sure way to get rid of demons is through the power of Jesus because He has all authority in the heavens and on earth. If a person is not full of the Spirit of Jesus, then how can they prevent demons from re-entering? So it is important, if we are to get free and live free, that we are filled with the Holy Spirit.

The last thing Jesus announced to His disciples before He ascended back to heaven was that they were to be filled with the Holy Spirit and with power (see Acts 1:8). Without Jesus' Holy Spirit, we are powerless against the enemy, but if we are full of the Holy Spirit, and in submission to Jesus, we have authority over every demon.

A retired soldier came into one of our Miracle Cafés and shared how he had suffered the debilitating pain of fibromyalgia and chronic fatigue for the past five years – it was a huge effort for this previously active man to even get out of bed and was badly affecting his quality of life, his relationship with God and his marriage. We explained that the conditions were likely caused by evil spirits, and then helped him as he confessed sin in his life and of coming into agreement with those demons. The Holy Spirit came powerfully upon him and the demons left instantly.

Immediately he knew he was healed, but he wrote to us later and told us that his life had completely changed from the moment he was set free and was filled with the Holy Spirit. Even his wife was saying she hardly recognized him, he was so changed for the better, and he was now healed and again living an active and fulfilled life. He shared his miracle story in his church and people who heard it were contacting us afterwards saying how they tangibly felt the presence and power of God as he was speaking, and could they have that too!

Expect to be transformed as you are set free and filled with the powerful Spirit of God.

"Be continually filled with the Holy Spirit... sing and make music in your heart to the Lord, always giving thanks to God the Father in everything, in the name of our Lord Jesus Christ" (Ephesians 5:18-20).

CHAPTER ELEVEN

Activation –
Time to Get Free!

I n this chapter I have included prayers that you can pray along with, that will help you to be set free from evil spirits. It's important before praying that you agree with the necessity to take the five steps (recognize, repent, renounce, remove, refill) from the previous chapter as this will ensure there are no blockages to your freedom.

Find a quiet place where you won't be disturbed. The prayers are not a formula, or an incantation, but they follow the guidelines I've previously mentioned according to the Bible; the Word of God. Jesus is the one who sets you free, not me. I am here to help you and guide you, that is all. Because of what Jesus accomplished when He died and rose from the dead, you can be free. It is through His blood and His authority and by the name of Jesus that Satan is defeated and demons have to leave, so always keep this in mind. It is not through any power of yours or mine, but because of Jesus the Anointed One.

You may want to be quiet for a few moments and let the Holy Spirit reveal how the enemy has been stealing from you and how he wants to destroy your life. Write down anything that comes to mind, as well as how you have come into agreement with those things. For example, it may seem odd, but ask yourself what you like about the addiction or negative behavior that torments you. This will be a clue as to what need the behavior is trying to replace. You may get a temporary feeling of love and acceptance, freedom or safety, but these are counterfeit feelings and agree with the lies of the enemy. Recognize them as such and utterly reject them in order to break the enemy's power over you so that you can come into true freedom.

We will begin by breaking off any agreement with the enemy's plans to bring you harm. Let's pray together:

Holy Spirit, please expose the plans of the enemy against my life. Lord God, shine the light of your presence in my heart and show me what I have said, done or thought that comes into agreement with those evil plans. Please reveal to me the patterns of thought and behavior, even things that I thought were part of my personality that are actually from the enemy. Please protect me from evil and lead me by your Holy Spirit.

1. RECOGNIZE

Thank you, Father God, for your love and your full acceptance of me. I believe that Jesus Christ is the Son of God and that He came to earth in the flesh and is the only way to God. Lord Jesus, thank you that you died on the cross for me and rose again from the dead. On the cross you took all my sin so that I might have right standing with God. Thank you, Jesus, that through your blood is the forgiveness of sins, healing and wholeness, freedom from demons and the gift of eternal life.

I recognize that I need you and I ask that you would set me free from the demons in my life and from all the powers of darkness that I have come into agreement with in any way throughout my life.

2. REPENT

I choose to surrender my life to you and I come before you now in humility. I ask for your light to shine in my heart and reveal to me all sin including secret, hidden and family sins. Help me to be honest and open. Thank you for your grace and mercy towards me.

Thank you that as I confess my sins, you choose to forgive me completely and remember them no more.

I confess the following sins from my past:

I confess these sins that I have been involved in recently:

I confess the following sins on behalf of my ancestors:

Father God, I thank you for your forgiveness of all my sins through the blood of your precious son, Jesus Christ.

To release yourself from any curse that may be on your life or family, I recommend you pray this out loud:

Jesus, you were made a curse so that I can be free from any curses that have come against me and my family, as well as the curse of sin and death that originated with Adam.

Please forgive me for any sin I have committed that has caused a curse to have power in my life and I choose to turn away from that sin. As I submit my life to you, I take authority over every curse that I have been living under whether that has come through my family generations, as a result of the occult, or from anything I have said, done or believed. Thank you for your forgiveness and I choose not to come into agreement with any plans of the enemy that are contrary to your plan for my life.

In the name of Jesus, I now release myself from every curse over my life – and going back through my generational line all the way back to Adam, and I tell it to leave me and my family and not to return. I commit my life to you, Jesus Christ and I ask that you would help me to continue to walk in freedom through your blood shed for me and through the power of your name. Amen.

3. RENOUNCE

I choose to turn away from all these sins and I renounce them in the name of Jesus. I choose to change my lifestyle where I need to, and my thinking.

I choose to forgive _____ for when they did or said _____ and for making me feel _____ and for all others who have wronged or harmed me, whether in action or words (Do this for each person who comes to mind).

In the name of Jesus I forgive them. Father God I receive your forgiveness for holding any bitterness (or anger or...) *in my heart towards _____ I pray that _____ would know you God and experience your love and freedom too.*

I separate myself from any false religion, New Age or occult practices, specifically _____ . I choose not to associate myself with these practices any longer and I cut myself off from any associated group. Lord, please give me wisdom to know how to do this and to choose new friends wisely. I commit to getting rid of any item in my possession that links me to past sins (Do this as soon as you get chance).

Thank you Jesus that you became a curse when you died on the cross, and I no longer need to live under the curse of original sin. Through your death and resurrection, every curse over my life is broken. By the blood of Jesus, I break every curse off my life and my family's life, whether it be a word curse, a blood curse, a spell, a dedication or any other curse from any source. Thank you, Father God for your blessings that I now receive.

4. REMOVE

Father God, please forgive me for coming into agreement with the enemy in any way. I renounce the lie that I am (unworthy, not wanted etc) _____ (or that I may get such and such disease etc) _____ *and I'm sorry that I have acted upon that lie by doing* _____ *or saying* _____ *and I command that demon and any symptoms or consequences connected with that demon to leave me now in the name of Jesus."*

And next we will confront specific demons that you have identified in your life. It doesn't matter if you don't know the name of the demon, it still has to leave.

I command the spirit of _____ (name the first demon on your list or any that the Holy Spirit shows you) *to leave in Jesus' name.*

Take a deep breath in of the Holy Spirit and breathe out or cough out the demon that you just commanded to leave. Keep breathing in with the Holy Spirit and out until that demon has gone. Then repeat this with each evil spirit until all have left. Some may take longer than others, but there's no reason why they can't all go quickly.

Keep breathing in the Holy Spirit and telling those evil spirits to leave.

GET FREE AND RECEIVE HEALING

As you do this you may notice things leaving you. You may realize you're making a noise or coughing, yawning or belching a lot. You may get a pain in your body or dizziness as the evil spirit leaves, your symptoms may temporarily worsen, or the pain may move around your body. These are all signs that it's an evil spirit and it's on its way out, so don't give up. If they speak to you and don't want to leave or tell you they're going to hurt you, don't be intimidated. Keep insisting they leave until they have all gone, and feel free to tell them to leave without causing you pain. They have to do as you tell them through the power of Jesus.

If you have any medical conditions or pain, you can pray this:

Father God, please forgive me for coming into agreement with any evil spirit that has caused _____ *(and then say what it is). Father God forgive me for coming into agreement with any evil spirit of* (pain, depression, despair, anxiety, addiction, cancer, arthritis etc) *when I spoke out _____ or took medication to try and suppress it.... or expected it to happen.... or gave in to fear...* (or whichever way you gave it a foothold in your life). *I'm sorry for believing the lies of the enemy over the Word of God and Your Truth. Whatever is causing this condition, I command that demonic spirit to leave me now through the power of Jesus who is the anointed one; the highest power.*

HOLY SPIRIT IN, DEMONS OUT!

Now take a deep breath in of the Holy Spirit and then on the count of three, cough out all evil spirits. ONE TWO THREE OUT!!!!! Breathe them out or cough them out, just get rid of them right now. As you do that, I release the power of the Lord Jesus and I take authority over every demon that is working in you right now and I tell that thing to leave and go to Jesus. Sense the presence of Jesus as this is happening. Thank you Jesus.

5. REFILL

We ask for the power of the Holy Spirit, the Spirit of Jesus Christ to fill you. Breathe in the Holy Spirit, out with the demons, in with the Holy Spirit.

Instead of the need for false affection, receive God's limitless love.

Instead of retreating into alcohol or drugs, be filled with the Holy Spirit.

Instead of seeking significance, receive your identity in Christ.

Instead of self-loathing, receive your crown of beauty.

Instead of guilt and shame, receive the forgiveness and acceptance of Jesus.

Instead of fear and anxiety, receive the Prince of Peace.

Instead of despair and heaviness, receive thankfulness and begin to praise Him.

Receive His joy - this should be fun, it's not a heavy thing. You're getting free and this is going to change your life! Honestly this has the potential to change your life, you don't need to be the same ever again. You can be healed now by being set free just as when Jesus performed miracles as He walked the earth and just like His disciples did.

Be at peace and completely free. Where the Spirit of the Lord is, there is FREEDOM.

Father God, thank you for your great love for me. Thank you for your forgiveness and freedom. Jesus, Anointed One, thank you that you came to earth as a man and surrendered your life for me. I choose to surrender my life to you and I ask you to come into my life and fill me with your powerful, wonderful Holy Spirit and your glory. Thank you that through you I am made brand new and this is a fresh start for me, a new beginning as a new creature, one with you!

Father God, I ask that you fill me to overflowing – baptize me with your precious Holy Spirit and lead me in your ways. In the name of the Lord Jesus Christ, Amen.

CHAPTER TWELVE

Stay Free

As we pursue a deeper knowledge of God and enjoy the fullness of life and purpose that He created us for, we can remain free. However, as we have already stated, Jesus warns us that after demons have left, they may try to return.

Evil spirits may attempt to come back into our lives after we have been set free, so it is imperative that we continue to surrender our hearts to Jesus and follow Him, continually being full of the Holy Spirit. It is only if we allow the enemy a foothold or open a door into our lives that he can enter.

If we initially invited demons into our lives by behaving or thinking a certain way, then of course, as we've already seen, we can be set free through the power of Jesus. But is it not likely that if the same behavior or thinking continues, then surely those same demons will simply return? This is why it is important that changes are made and we do not continue to live as we once did.

If you have been healed and you begin to experience symptoms again, or if you had unhealthy thoughts or patterns of behavior and those thoughts try and return, it could simply be an evil spirit trying its luck! So straight away tell it to stop at the name of Jesus and DO NOT come into agreement with it in any way. Once you have done this, the demon will leave you alone, although it may try and return at another time in the future, so always be focused on Jesus and full of His Spirit and joy and choose not to give those cheeky evil spirits any place in your life in the future.

"Your eye is the lamp of your body. When your eyes are healthy, your whole body also is full of light. But when they are unhealthy, your body also is full of darkness. See to it, then, that the light within you is not darkness. Therefore, if your whole body is full of light, and no part of it dark, it will be just as full of light as when a lamp shines its light on you" (Luke 11:34-36).

The more we can remain full of the presence of Jesus and His glory, and follow His ways, being led by His Spirit, the less likely we are to succumb to evil spirits.

BETTER THE DEVIL YOU KNOW?

It can be quick and easy to get free, like a prisoner being released from jail; suddenly we are out and in the fresh air. However, now we have new independence and responsibilities (which may seem a little daunting at first) so it will require determination and resolve to learn how to live outside of the prison. We may have been thinking toxic thoughts about ourselves and others for many years, so it may take time to 'reprogram our thought life' (and be transformed in our minds). Otherwise, tragically, like an institution-alized prisoner, we may decide it's harder to live on the outside and sabotage our freedom (reoffend) to go back to the familiar prison, albeit one of suffering.

BE FOCUSED, NOT DRIVEN

The enemy tries to get us off course by causing us to give up on our walk with God and our purpose in Him, but if he cannot do that, he will try and distract us. One of the ways he does this is through our work or even our Christian ministry. We need to have the humility to recognize when we are serving other motivations in ministry rather than serving the Lord. The enemy may cause us to be so driven in trying to achieve our goals that we burn ourselves out. From his point of view this is just as effective as making us give up. The key is to be focussed on serving the Lord in faith and not driven to succeed in our own strength.

Other times, the enemy will use relationships to cause us to move away from our purpose and from the abiding place of rest in God. It could be a person who has first place in our affections, or perhaps an annoying colleague, a bully, criticism from others and so on. Do not be distracted. Our fight is not against flesh and blood, so always be quick to forgive and ask the Lord for the humility to let it go. The devil hates humility because it actually makes our relationship with the Lord stronger; so he has to give up the attack.

We can ask the Holy Spirit to give us discernment and to see the spirit behind the behavior or the situation and deal with that. Follow the way of love when dealing with people, but don't give evil spirits a foothold. The devil is our enemy, not people.

How do we react when a crisis emerges? We are all faced with challenging situations from time to time, but it is how we react that is important. The enemy wants to cause a response in us that will bring anxiety and turmoil. It is important not to live in response to the devil. We can learn from Jesus when He was faced with a crisis. He heard that one of his close friends, Lazarus, was very sick and on the point of death. However, the crisis did not alter His schedule. He stayed where He was for two days before going to visit Lazarus, who by this point had already died. Jesus was not moved by crisis, but went on to raise Lazarus to life, back from the dead. Jesus told us that He only did and spoke what He saw His Father doing (see John 5:19). Now that is how I would love to live, wouldn't you?

Another way the enemy seeks to get us off track is by using politics or even current news items. He wants to bring fear and anxiety into our lives and he aims to bring division between family relationships and against friends. I have noticed on social media that even 'Christians' attack each other and display hatred towards others simply because they have a differing political or theological viewpoint. I try and steer clear of politics on my social media but even so, I've had death threats from so-called Christians who have turned my miracle stories or encouraging posts into an opportunity to attack me and others. It's crazy and so demonic and its aim is to distract and divide. Beware of getting into arguments like this – it really is pointless and is an open door to evil spirits.

Once we have been set free from a demon it is our responsibility to make right choices and to prevent that evil spirit from coming back in.

YOUR TRUE IDENTITY

Recently as I was reading Ephesians, the Lord high-lighted to me how the message of that whole book can help us stay free from demons, so I encourage you to read it for yourself. However, I will highlight some passages here to help you get the revelation of who you really are and what authority and power is within you as you surrender your life to Jesus.

In Biblical times, a son and heir in a family would, at a certain age, come to maturity and would be given the same standing and authority as his father. When a person was doing business with the son, it was just as though they were doing business with his father, as he carried the same authority. If that son was to rebel and leave the family, he would no longer carry his father's authority.

Incredibly, in the first chapter of Ephesians, we read how God has chosen us to be His mature 'sons', receiving His full inheritance and carrying His authority, as we remain in Him. In fact, the Greek word in this passage for 'adoption' means 'the placing of a mature son':

"...He chose us in Him before the creation of the world to be holy and blameless in His sight. In love He predestined us for adoption to sonship through Jesus Christ, in accordance with His pleasure and will— to the praise of His glorious grace, which He has freely given us in the One He loves. In Him we have redemption through His blood, the forgiveness of sins, in accordance with the riches of God's grace that He lavished on us" (Ephesians 1:4-8).

I pray that any veil the enemy has used to try and cover your mind from understanding these truths will be removed as you read and absorb these powerful words. It is time for you to hope again and to know the full inheritance available to you through Jesus.

"I keep asking that the God of our Lord Jesus Christ, the glorious Father, may give you the Spirit of wisdom and revelation, so that you may know Him better. I pray that the eyes of your heart may be enlightened in order that you may know the hope to which He has called you, the riches of His glorious inheritance in His holy people, and His incomparably great power for us who believe" (Ephesians 1:17-19).

It is important that we, as children of God, receive the Spirit of revelation so that we can know God and who He really is. He wants to reveal to us the full inheritance that is available as we believe and step into our new identity as His mature sons. He wants to give us and reveal through us, the riches of His glory and power over all that is subject to Him. We cannot have authority over demons unless we surrender to Jesus. As we do this, we are able to receive the revelation of who He is and what He has accomplished, and subsequently who we really are and the authority and power we carry when we live in Him.

Chapter two of Ephesians goes on to describe our previous life under the power of Satan:

"As for you, you were dead in your transgressions and sins, in which you used to live when you followed the ways of this world and of the ruler of

the kingdom of the air, the spirit who is now at work in those who are disobedient. All of us also lived among them at one time, gratifying the cravings of our flesh and following its desires and thoughts. Like the rest, we were by nature deserving of wrath" (Ephesians 2:1-3).

But this passage continues with the truth of what happens when we surrender our lives and become one with Jesus:

"Because of His great love for us, God, who is rich in mercy, made us alive with Christ even when we were dead in transgressions—it is by grace you have been saved. And God raised us up with Christ and seated us with Him in the heavenly realms in Christ Jesus" (Ephesians 2:4-6).

This is so good. So if and when the enemy tries to come back and attempts to bring you down to his level, just remember that you are in Christ Jesus, far and above all powers and principalities of darkness. So if we believe, trust in and follow Jesus Christ, then He brings us true life and takes us up into heavenly places with Him, far above the ruler of the kingdom of the air; Satan and his demons. That is a key right there to your new life of freedom. I hope you're getting this!

Chapter three of Ephesians goes on to say:

"His intent was that now, through the church (followers of Jesus who know who they are), the manifold wisdom of God should be made known to the rulers and authorities in the heavenly realms, according to His eternal purpose that He accomplished in Christ Jesus our Lord. In Him and through faith in Him we may approach God with freedom and confidence" (Ephesians 3:10-12).

"I pray that out of His glorious riches He may strengthen you with power through His Spirit in your inner being, so that Christ may dwell in your hearts through faith. And I pray that you, being rooted and established in love, may have power, together with all the Lord's holy people, to grasp how wide and long and high and deep is the love of Christ, and to know this love that surpasses knowledge – that you may be filled to the measure of all the fullness of God" (Ephesians 3:16-19).

God loves you so much and He delights in you. Your past is in the past and He has forgiven you. The Bible says that God chooses to remember our sin no more, so if you have asked Him to forgive you, but still feel guilt and shame, then that is likely to be the enemy, so just tell him to jog on! Then thank God for what He has done for you. You have a clean slate.

Ephesians chapter four instructs us in a better way of living so that we can walk in freedom. I'm tempted to quote the whole chapter, but here's a portion of it. I've added in headings for you:

KEEP YOUR HEART SOFT

"So I tell you this, and insist on it in the Lord, that you must no longer live as the Gentiles do, in the futility of their thinking. They are darkened in their understanding and separated from the life of God because of the ignorance that is in them due to the hardening of their hearts. Having lost all sensitivity, they have given themselves over to sensuality so as to indulge in every kind of impurity, and they are full of greed" (Ephesians 4:17-19).

YOU ARE CREATED TO BE LIKE GOD

"That, however, is not the way of life you learned when you heard about Christ and were taught in Him in accordance with the truth that is in Jesus. You were taught, with regard to your former way of life, to put off your old self, which is being corrupted by its deceitful desires; to be made new in the attitude of your minds; and to put on the new self, created to be like God in true righteousness and holiness" (Ephesians 4:20-24).

WAYS THE ENEMY WILL TRY AND GET IN

"Therefore each of you must put off falsehood and

speak truthfully to your neighbor, for we are all members of one body. 'In your anger do not sin': do not let the sun go down while you are still angry, and do not give the devil a foothold. Anyone who has been stealing must steal no longer, but must work, doing something useful with their own hands, that they may have something to share with those in need.

Do not let any unwholesome talk come out of your mouths, but only what is helpful for building others up according to their needs, that it may benefit those who listen. And do not grieve the Holy Spirit of God, with whom you were sealed for the day of redemption. Get rid of all bitterness, rage and anger, brawling and slander, along with every form of malice. Be kind and compassionate to one another, forgiving each other, just as in Christ God forgave you" (Ephesians 4:17-32).

CHILDREN OF LIGHT

Getting free from evil spirits is so liberating and gives us a fresh start from which to recognize the ways of darkness so we can make the right choices each day. We can embrace all that God has for us as we continue to live in the light.

"For you were once darkness, but now you are light in the Lord. Live as children of light (for the fruit of the light consists in all goodness, righteousness and truth). Have nothing to do with the fruitless deeds of darkness, but rather expose them. It is shameful even to mention what the disobedient do in secret. But everything exposed by the light becomes visible – and everything that is illuminated becomes a light" (Ephesians 5:8-9, 11-13).

YOU ARE MORE POWERFUL THAN YOU THOUGHT!

In the final chapter of Ephesians, the Apostle Paul exhorts us to put on spiritual armor because we are mighty warriors in a spiritual battle. I have changed the tense so that you can read this aloud:

"I will be strong in the Lord and in His mighty power. I put on the full armor of God, so that I can take my stand against the devil's schemes... not against flesh and blood, but against the rulers, against the authorities, against the powers of this dark world and against the spiritual forces of evil in the heavenly realms... I stand firm with the belt of truth buckled around my waist, with the breastplate of righteousness in place, and with my feet fitted with the readiness that comes from the gospel of peace. In addition to all this, I take up the shield of faith, with which I can extinguish all the flaming arrows of the evil one. I take the helmet of salvation and the sword of the Spirit, which is the word of

God. Lord, help me to pray in the Spirit on all occasions as you have instructed me" (Ephesians 6:12-18).

I encourage you to read the whole book of Ephesians. You may want to meditate on and memorize some of those powerful verses. 'Eating' the Word of God in this way brings nourishment to your soul and has the power to transform your life.

POWERFUL WEAPONS

In all we do, it is good to remain in a place of rest and in peace. Peace is a powerful weapon and one which the enemy tries to take from us. Resist him, and do not succumb to fear or anxiety. Walk in peace at all times. **"The God of peace will crush Satan under my feet"** **(Romans 16:20).**

THE MIGHTY POWER THAT SAVES US

I have included another Scripture here which wonderfully speaks of God coming to our rescue and delivering us from our enemy Satan. You may want to read this out as a prayer.

"I love you, Yahweh, and I'm bonded to you, my strength! Yahweh, you're the bedrock beneath my feet, my faith-fortress, my wonderful deliverer, my God, my rock of rescue where none can reach me.

You're the shield around me, the mighty power that saves me, and my high place. All I need to do is to call on you, Yahweh, the praiseworthy God. When I do, I'm safe and sound in you - delivered from my foes! For when the cords of death wrapped around me and torrents of destruction overwhelmed me, taking me to death's door, in my distress I cried out to you, the delivering God, and from your temple-throne you heard my troubled cry, and my sobs went right into your heart...

Suddenly the brilliance of His presence broke through with lightning bolts and hail—a tempest dropping coals of fire. The Lord thundered; the great God above every god spoke with His thunder-voice from the sky. The Most High uttered His voice! He released His lightning-arrows, and routed my foes. See how they ran and scattered in fear!...

He rescued me from the mighty waters and drew me to Himself! Even though I was helpless in the hands of my hateful, strong enemy, you were good to deliver me. When I was at my weakest, my enemies attacked—but the Lord held on to me. His love broke open the way, and He brought me into a beautiful, broad place. He rescued me—because His delight is in me! He rewarded me for doing what's right and staying pure. I will follow His commands and I'll not sin by ceasing to follow Him, no matter what" (Psalms 18:1-21).

What a wonderful picture this is, of God seeing us in our trouble and coming to our rescue. This is what He has done for us, for you, as you call on His name and follow Him with all your heart. As the last verse says, keep doing what is right and staying pure. The only way to do this is by following Him with all your heart. Make that choice today and every day, to keep following Him no matter what. Choose to trust Him in all things and as you do this, you will be able to stay free and be kept safe from harm.

CHAPTER THIRTEEN

A New You!

Know that you are loved by God; you are His child and continue walking in the light. As soon as the light comes, darkness has to flee.

NO LIMITS

Luke 8:2 tells how Jesus had a close group of friends and followers: **"And the twelve were with Him, and also some women who had been healed of evil spirits and infirmities: Mary, called Magdalene, from whom seven demons had gone out..."** This passage wonderfully shows how Jesus not only welcomes those who have a 'past' but some of His closest followers and friends were demonized until Jesus set them free. He didn't seem to place any restrictions on what any of them could or couldn't do.

I want you to know that you are loved by God and nothing in your past can prevent you from fulfilling your destiny in God; not even all the demons of hell.

As you become free, don't look back, but keep your eyes fixed on Jesus and don't let anything try to stop you from living the life you were born for. You are perfect in Him, free from guilt and accusation.

"If anyone is in Christ, he is a new creation; the old has gone, the new has come!" (2 Corinthians 5:17).

Let's make it personal: **"I am in Christ. I am a new creation. The old me has gone and the new me is here!"**

THE IMPORTANCE OF BAPTISM

When we choose to follow Jesus, we choose to surrender our own will and our old lifestyle, letting go of our past and stepping into a new existence in Jesus. We choose to obey Him and be led by His Holy Spirit. We go from the kingdom of darkness into the kingdom of light – we receive the forgiveness of sins and become part of God's family.

Baptism in water by full immersion is the outward physical sign of what has happened to us spiritually and is an important part of our new life. "Whoever believes and is baptized will be saved…" (Mark 16:16). This word 'saved' in its original meaning means 'saved from sin and eternal damnation, healed, set free from demons, kept safe and made whole.'

"...This water symbolizes baptism that now saves you also – not the removal of dirt from the body but the pledge of a clear conscience towards God. It saves you by the resurrection of Jesus Christ, who has gone into heaven and is at God's right hand – with angels, authorities and powers in submission to Him" (1 Peter 3:21-22).

We have often found as we baptize new believers, that demons leave as the person comes up out of the water, and the Holy Spirit fills the person at the same time. It is very powerful. Many of those we have baptized tell us later that addictions and harmful thoughts left and they have been completely free of that thing since.

So I would encourage everyone who chooses to follow Jesus to be baptized by full immersion in water as soon as is practical.

"...All of us who were baptized into Christ Jesus were baptized into His death. We were therefore buried with Him through baptism into death in order that, just as Christ was raised from the dead through the glory of the Father, we too may live a new life. For if we have been united with Him in a death like His, we will certainly also be united with Him in a resurrection like His. For we know that our old self was crucified with Him so that the body ruled by sin might be done away with, that we should no longer be slaves to sin – because anyone who has died has been set free from sin" (Romans 6:3-7).

RIGHT PRIORITIES

The Bible says to **"Seek first the kingdom of God"** – that's Jesus and His rule and reign – **"and His righteousness"**, and as we do that, we will find that everything else in our life falls into place.

We have been created in God's image to bring Him glory by revealing His glory on earth. We are new creation beings and what we have now is even better than what Adam and Eve had in the garden before they sinned. The devil wants to stop that. He cannot bear the fact that we are loved by God and we are joint heirs with Jesus, inheriting all that He is and has.

"So then, just as you received Christ Jesus as Lord, continue to live your lives in Him, rooted and built up in Him, strengthened in the faith as you were taught, and overflowing with thankfulness. See to it that no-one takes you captive through hollow and deceptive philosophy, which depends on human tradition and the elemental spiritual forces of this world rather than on Christ. For in Christ all the fullness of the Deity lives in bodily form, and in Christ you have been brought to fullness. He is the head over every power and authority" (Colossians 2:6-10).

MADE IN THE IMAGE OF GOD

Noemi, whom I mentioned earlier, explained that if

we let other people's opinions of us affect us, say through social media or something spoken to us that is not true, it is akin to looking into a distorted mirror like those at the funfair where the image we see is a crazy reflection of the real us. What we are receiving is other people's fears, weaknesses or worldview and believing it to be our true identity, when in fact it is nothing more than a lie of the enemy and not who we really are. Instead, let God be our mirror and believe what He says about us and thinks of us.

"But whenever someone turns to the Lord, the veil is taken away… So all of us who have had that veil removed can see as though looking in a mirror and reflect the glory of the Lord. And the Lord—who is the Spirit—makes us more and more like Him as we are changed into His glorious image" (2 Corinthians 3:16,18 NLT).

The devil wants to deceive us into thinking that our problems are due to something bad that has happened in our past and he will incite us to blame others. For example, you may have ended up believing you were inadequate because nothing you ever did seemed good enough for your parents. In adulthood you realize that this has led to a raft of negative beliefs about yourself. This in turn can lead to a lack of forgiveness, becoming bitter and wanting revenge. Having a victim mentality keeps us under the power of the devil, not being able to move forward with our lives.

Instead, let's use any challenges we face to drive us deeper into God. In the Bible, we read how Joseph's brothers tried to kill him and he wound up being ill-treated and imprisoned unfairly. However, Joseph did not become bitter towards them: **"You intended to harm me, but God intended it for good" (Genesis 50:20).** Because he remained humble and did not seek revenge, God's purposes were accomplished. As a result, Joseph was given the highest place in the land next to the King and was able to save thousands of lives. Amazingly, he was also reconciled with his family.

So, I encourage you to not let your past challenges or failures dictate your future but choose to live in freedom and joy, fulfilling your destiny as a beloved child of God.

Your life from now on can be very different from how it was, and if you want a fresh start you can! Change your outlook and embrace life. If you continue to see yourself as a victim or sick or an addict or whatever label you put on yourself, you will always be a victim or always sick or addicted, and wonder why people always treat you in a certain way.

But you are free to make changes now. If you want a happy marriage, be the one who is happy; be content. If you want to be trusted, be trustworthy. If you want to be loved, then be lovable. Love others and treat them as you would like to be treated. If you want to be healed, then be healthy. Pray for others to be healed too, and so on.

The Bible says we can be transformed by renewing our minds, so let's focus on all that is pure and wholesome and lovely and keep in mind the things of God. **"As a man thinks, so he is" (Proverbs 23:7).**

Instead of going after what I want, or what I think I need, let's be led by the Holy Spirit in all things and not be controlled by needs and wants. What a difference that will make.

BE GENEROUS

When Rob and I were first married, like many young couples, we took out loans to pay for things like a washing machine, towards a car and we also took on the biggest mortgage we could afford. However, we got into difficulties as interest rates soared to 15% and house prices plummeted. It got to a point where the cash machine swallowed our bank cards and we didn't even have enough money for food. Sadly, we didn't learn our lesson, and a few years later a similar thing happened, but this time the debts were huge and our world came crashing down.

We chose to throw ourselves on God, and thankfully, letting go of our dreams, we followed exactly what the Holy Spirit told us to do, and we dramatically got out of debt. It involved making some tough decisions, but at that point we chose to never get into debt again, and we haven't, all these years later. We started to give to others, even when we had next to nothing, and we soon discovered that giving was the way to break the power of a poverty spirit.

To walk in freedom, do the opposite of the demonic spirit. Instead of hate, love. Be a giver, not a taker, and be free. In this way we can live from a superior reality; a heavenly reality.

"Since we are His true children, we qualify to share all His treasures, for indeed, we are heirs of God Himself. And since we are joined to Christ, we also inherit all that He is and all that He has, as joint heirs" (Romans 8:17).

Remember, **"He who is in you is greater than he who is in the world" (1 John 4:4).**

CHAPTER FOURTEEN

Be The Light

"Jesus addressed the crowd. He said, "I am the Light of the world. He who follows me will not walk in the darkness, but will have the Light of life" (John 8:12).

Jesus is the light and not only that: when we surrender our life to Him, we too become the light.

"You're here to be light, bringing out the God-colors in the world. God is not a secret to be kept. We're going public with this, as public as a city on a hill. If I make you light-bearers, you don't think I'm going to hide you under a bucket, do you? I'm putting you on a light stand. Now that I've put you there on a hilltop, on a light-stand – shine!" (Matthew 5:14-16 MSG).

"For you were once darkness, but now you are light in the Lord. Live as children of light" (Ephesians 5:8).

This is your time to shine; in fact you were born for

this! The light has come into your life and as you continue to shine with the glory of Jesus, darkness cannot remain. Darkness is all around, but you are the light and the light is more powerful than the darkness. So instead of coming under feelings of depression or anxiety or whatever is going on around you, know that you are the light and through Jesus, you have power over all darkness. You can impact the atmosphere, no matter where you are or who you are with. We are the revelation of Jesus unveiled on the earth.

ARISE AND SHINE

There are so many Scriptures that I love, and Isaiah 60 is no exception. The Amplified translation of the first few verses is powerful. Read this slowly, as an exhortation to you from the Lord:

"Arise [from spiritual depression to a new life], shine [be radiant with the glory and brilliance of the Lord]; for your light has come, and the glory and brilliance of the Lord has risen upon you. For in fact, darkness will cover the earth and deep darkness will cover the peoples; but the Lord will rise upon you and His glory and brilliance will be seen on you. Nations will come to your light, and kings to the brightness of your rising. Lift up your eyes around you and see; they all gather together, they come to you. Your sons will come from far away, and your daughters will be looked after at their side. Then

you will see and be radiant, and your heart will tremble [with joy] and rejoice" (Isaiah 60:1-5 AMP).

These verses promise that as we rise up and shine with God's glory, we attract others to Him and we will become full of joy.

Under the Old Covenant, Moses would glow so brightly after being in God's presence, that he had to wear a veil over his face. In the opening chapter of this book, I shared how the enemy blinds our minds and our souls with a veil so we are unable to know the truth. But as we embrace Jesus' death and resurrection in our own lives, that veil is removed.

"We can all draw close to Him with the veil removed from our faces. And with no veil we all become like mirrors who brightly reflect the glory of the Lord Jesus. We are being transfigured into His very image as we move from one brighter level of glory to another. And this glorious transfiguration comes from the Lord, who is the Spirit" (2 Corinthians 3:18 TPT).

The Apostle Paul contrasts the transforming power of the old covenant with that of the new. He told of how Moses' face shone with the glory of God but how it had faded over time, even though it was hidden by a veil. In contrast, the light reflected in our faces from the Lord's glory is ever increasing as we go from one degree of radiance to another! (see 2 Corinthians 3:7-11).

What Moses concealed, we are to reveal. In these days I believe we will see more and more followers of Jesus glowing with His glory.

"For God, who said, 'Let light shine out of darkness,' made His light shine in our hearts to give us the light of the knowledge of the glory of God in the face of Christ" (2 Corinthians 4:6).

SHINE BRIGHT

Jesus gave us a glimpse of the brightness of God's glory revealed in a human body, even before His death and resurrection. When Jesus walked the earth as a man, He often climbed up a mountain to spend time with Father God alone. One time, He took His three closest friends with Him and they were privileged to witness an incredible event; a cloud surrounded them and God spoke: **"This is my Son, whom I love; with Him I am well pleased. Listen to Him!"**

Jesus' face and clothes 'transfigured' and began to shine with such luminosity that the disciples could not look at Him; the Bible tells us He was glowing as brightly as the sun (see Luke 9).

BE TRANSFORMED

The Greek word in the original text used here for

'transfigured' is 'metamorphoo' which means to change into another form. It is where we get our word 'metamorphosis' which is the word used to describe the complete transformation of a caterpillar into a beautiful butterfly.

That Greek word is also found in Romans 12:2: **"Do not conform to the pattern of this world, but be transformed by the renewing of your mind..."**

Interestingly, 'metamorphoo' is also used in 2 Corinthians 3:18: **"And we all, who with unveiled faces contemplate the Lord's glory, are being transformed into His image with ever-increasing glory, which comes from the Lord, who is the Spirit."**

So, as we keep our focus on Jesus, on bringing Him glory and remaining IN Him, our minds are renewed and we are increasingly transformed, transfigured and literally begin to shine and glow as we radiate and release His glory, everywhere we go.

REVEAL GOD'S GLORY AND DEMONS FLEE

Let's go back to the transfiguration account of Jesus on the mountainside. The very next day, after the glory had emanated from Jesus so brightly, we read that the group came down from the mountain to a great crowd of people. There they encountered a demonized boy and the desperate cries of his father:

"'Please, Teacher, I beg of you, do something about my son, my only son. An evil spirit possesses him and makes him scream out in torment, and hardly ever leaves him alone. It throws him into convulsions and he foams at the mouth. When it finally does leave him, he's left with horrible bruises...' Then He said to the man, 'Bring your son to me.' As the boy approached, the demon slammed him to the ground and threw him into violent convulsions. Jesus sternly commanded the demon to come out of the boy, and it left immediately. Jesus healed the boy of his injuries and returned him to his father, saying, 'Here is your son'" (Luke 9:37-42 TPT).

Just like Jesus modelled for us here, we too are called to walk in the power of God's glory as we encounter others who require freedom and wholeness. As we have been forgiven and set free by Him, we in turn do likewise and help set others free.

It's simple really: Jesus surrendered His life (including His will and all His rights) so that He could live in us. We surrender our lives (including our will and all our rights) to Him so that He can reveal His glory in and through us. The more we surrender to Him and follow Him, the more His glory will be revealed in us and impact the world around us.

LET'S LIVE IN THE SHINING PLACE

"Yahweh, who dares to dwell with you? Who presumes the privilege of being close to you, living next to you in your shining place of glory? They are passionate and wholehearted, always sincere and always speaking the truth, for their hearts are trustworthy. They refuse to slander or insult others; they'll never listen to gossip or rumors, nor would they ever harm a friend with their words. They will despise evil and evil workers while commending the faithful ones who follow after the truth. They make firm commitments and follow through, even at great cost. They never crush others with exploitation and they would never be bought with a bribe against the innocent. Those who do these things will never be shaken; they will stand firm forever" (Psalm 15:1-5 TPT).

This is our inheritance and once we step into this new way of living, which is a far superior reality to our old life, even creation is impacted:

"The entire universe is standing on tiptoe, yearning to see the unveiling of God's glorious sons and daughters made known" (Romans 8:19).

Let us keep our eyes fixed on Jesus. At the end of this age that we find ourselves living in, the Living God is exposing the devil and his schemes and unveiling His sons and daughters in all their glory (that's you and me)! In and through you, God wants to uncover and shine His light which overpowers the darkness, and reveal His truth, helping others to understand and apply it to their own lives. We are in the last days and it is time for us to live in the fullness of this inheritance with Jesus.

AS YOU GO...

Jesus gave His followers authority and sent them out to spread the good news of the amazing truth of God's kingdom: **"As you go, proclaim this message: 'The kingdom of heaven has come near.' Heal the sick, raise the dead, cleanse those who have leprosy, drive out demons. Freely you have received; freely give" (Matthew 10:7).**

"When the seventy missionaries returned to Jesus, they were ecstatic with joy, telling him, "Lord, even the demons obeyed us when we commanded them in your name!" Jesus replied, "While you were ministering, I watched Satan topple until he fell suddenly from heaven like lightning to the ground. Now you understand that I have imparted to you my authority to trample over his kingdom.

You will trample upon every demon before you and overcome every power Satan possesses. Absolutely nothing will harm you as you walk in this authority.

However, your real source of joy isn't merely that these spirits submit to your authority, but that YOUR NAMES ARE WRITTEN IN THE JOURNALS OF HEAVEN and that YOU BELONG TO GOD'S KINGDOM. This is the true source of your authority" (Luke 10:17-20 TPT).

No matter what crazy things you witness as you go about your Heavenly Father's business, remember this: you belong to God, you are His child and you are a joint heir with Jesus, in God's kingdom family. You are called to be a bright, shining one, full of the Spirit of God, living in freedom and wholeness, releasing light as you demonstrate God's love and power everywhere you go.

"The lovers of God walk on the highway of light, the glow of the sunlight of dawn, and their way shines brighter and brighter until the perfect day" (Proverbs 4:18).

It is important to find others who are seeking to walk in the light of Jesus. It is easy to slip back into old ways of thinking and being, particularly if we do not have others around us to encourage us. We recommend you seek out a Holy Spirit-filled local church or online community for support, equipping and encouragement in your spiritual walk. There are many wonderful ones out there although we would of course also love you to join our online community. We have powerful training videos and activations as well as online and local Classes in many nations (details are on the following pages). The important thing is to connect with other followers of Jesus and go where you will grow and where the Holy Spirit leads.

"Fill your thoughts with my words
until they penetrate deep into your spirit.
Then, as you unwrap my words,
they will impart true life and radiant health
into the very core of your being.
So above all, guard the affections of your heart,
for they affect all that you are.
Pay attention to the welfare of your innermost
being,
for from there flows the wellspring of life.
Avoid dishonest speech and pretentious words.
Be free from using perverse words no matter what!
Set your gaze on the path before you.
With fixed purpose, looking straight ahead,
ignore life's distractions.
Watch where you're going!
Stick to the path of truth,
and the road will be safe and smooth before you.
Don't allow yourself to be sidetracked for even a
moment
or take the detour that leads to darkness"
(Proverbs 4:21-27 TPT).

The purpose from the outset was that God's glory, the

manifest presence of Jesus would be revealed and visibly recognized throughout the earth. When we take our place and shine, His glory will become known everywhere we go. We are the revelation of Jesus Christ unveiled on the earth as we release His light in this dark world and shine with His glory; brighter and brighter until all darkness is gone, in the kingdom of His light.

www.SpiritLifestyle.org

If you have been impacted by this book, I would love to hear about your experience!

Follow @alisscresswell:

Facebook, YouTube & Podcast

More Books from
Rob & Aliss Cresswell

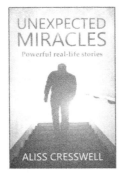

SpiritLifestyle.org

miracle.cafe®

a taste of heaven

global network

SpiritLifestyle.org

Printed in Great Britain
by Amazon

24881046R00150